Integrating Experiential and Brief Therapy

HOW TO DO DEEP THERAPY - BRIEFLY
and
HOW TO DO BRIEF THERAPY - DEEPLY

A Guide for Therapists, Counselors and Clients

Second Edition

Bala Jaison, Ph.D.

Second Edition of:
Integrating Experiential and Brief Therapy
How To Do Deep Therapy – Briefly and How To Do Brief Therapy – Deeply (2004)

Library and Archives Canada Cataloguing in Publication

Jaison, Bala
Integrating experiential and brief therapy : how to do deep therapy - briefly and how to do brief therapy - deeply : a guide for therapists, counselors and clients / Bala Jaison. -- 2nd ed.

Includes bibliographical references.
ISBN 978-0-9732286-2-5

1. Psychotherapy. 2. Experiential psychotherapy.
3. Brief psychotherapy. 4. Psychotherapy--Case studies.
I. Title.

RC480.J34 2007 616.89'14
C2006-906157-2
Printed in Canada

Book Cover by Valeriy Zevin
Art and Design by Ken MacDonald

Praise for *Integrating Experiential and Brief Therapy...*

I love this book! It is brilliant in its simplicity, clear and accurate, showing exactly where the two approaches meet, differ, and cross.

Dr. Erna de Bruijn, M.D.
The Netherlands

The book is like a breath of fresh air! - readable, concrete, and immediately applicable. It's a terrifically accessible tool ... direct, simple, and humorous. It really works. I particularly appreciate how it embodies these two seeming disparate practices, into a workable and powerful whole that makes sense.

Karen Whalen, Ph.D.
York University, Toronto

Family medicine practice and training have come to rely on brief psychotherapy strategies as a means of accommodating a large volume of patients who are in immediate need. I have come to rely on this timely, clearly written, and very valuable resource in my own practice and in the training of other physicians and residents.

Pauline Pariser, M.Asc., M.D., C.C.F.P.
Toronto, Canada

Your book is fabulous! I've already referred to certain sections for use with particular clients. I really like the four Interventions, especially the "Miracle Question". Wanted to mention the Fifth Intervention - your book is the "Miracle Answer"! How did I ever live without it?

Carole G. Pentony, Ph.D.
Clinical Psychologist
Houston, Texas

Dr. Jaison's book is an invaluable resource when I teach physicians strategies in psychotherapy. It gives a clear and practical approach to the integration of solution-focused strategies with experiential psychotherapy. I recommend that all psychotherapists read this book.

Mel Borins, M.D.
Assistant Professor
Faculty of Medicine
University of Toronto

Table of Contents

Acknowledgements

My heartfelt thanks…

First to two cherished friends and colleagues. On the Focusing side, to my soul-sister, Dr. Joan Klagsbrun: For your profound clinical wisdom, insight, and skilled feed-back – not to mention unwavering support and unconditional love. Your belief in me kept me going. Thank you.

On the Solution side: To my treasured colleague, Andrea Halperin, MSW. Your clinical brilliance never fails to astound me. Your editing suggesting and writing assistance were invaluable…you saw so much that I missed and filled in the blanks. I'm forever grateful.

To Gene Gendlin: Thank you…for being a mentor, friend, listener, and for giving me hours and hours of time to pick your brains. You taught me how to listen to myself in very new ways. I sincerely hope that I have done justice to your work.

To Dr. Mary McGuire: There are no words…from you I learned 'more' than Focusing. I learned everything about love. Thank you forever.

To the Solution Folks: Insoo Kim Berg for ongoing inspiration; Bill O'Hanlon for widening my scope with "possibilities"; Jim Duvall for helping me stay Solution Focused; Millie Greenfield for giving me confidence in myself. To Eric King: Thank you first and foremost for your sensitive supervision and willingness to let me include affective components into a Brief Therapy interview. And now, all these years later, for giving me the final and very subtle finishing touches. Thank you.

To Dr. Glenn Fleisch: Through the process of co-thinking and subsequently co-teaching, the acronym SOFT (Solution Oriented Focusing Therapy) evolved. The word has wonderful meaning and great memories for me of our work together. Thank you.

To Ruth Buczynski: For the brilliant idea of transcribing my workshop for you. The transcription turned out to be the spine in the body of this book - everything else stemmed from that. Thank you so much for the inspiration.

To Marc Rosen: Your vision of what would make it better was extraordinary. Your patience with the minutest details makes you the great editor that you are. Your commitment was unwavering. Thank you profoundly.

To Ken Mac Donald: Your artwork, your editing suggestions, the time and caring you put into this project made it come alive. You saw it visually in a way that I couldn't, and kept perspective that I lost after the 100th edit! Thank you.

To Valery Zevin: A double thank you. First, for the new redesigned book cover. We are so often on the visual 'same page'. Second, for being my "Mac Genius". You helped keep me sane when nothing would work due to "technical difficulties". Thank you.

To Dawn Kasten: You managed to interpret my cartoon 'vision' of Focusing, exactly as I had imagined it. Your artistic talent is awesome! Thank you.

To John O'Shea: We started our connection with "stuff-it" and ended with Job (like the Bible not the work!) Yes, it has been a test to the limit! Your computer savvy alone is worth an Academy Award. Your impeccable patience is a gift worthy of… Job, of course! Thank you for pulling this together.

To Bob Waller: Talk about "P's & Q's". Thank you for the final grammatical touches.

Special thanks to my family for all the time I was 'somewhere else', and loving me anyway. My love back to you.

Dedication

This book is dedicated to all the clinicians, both known and unknown, who listen to their clients with care and attention, hour after hour, and day after day, with one essential goal in mind: To help, to serve, and to heal. I sincerely hope the following gives you another useful tool for your clinical grab-bag!

In The Beginning...

Since what I have to say here is in no particular order, I'll do the 'experiential thing' and start where I am, right now, in the moment…I have wanted to write this book for a very long time. In fact, I wanted to write it even before I had enough information to write it, if that makes any sense…maybe that is the beginning.

I have been practicing Focusing Oriented Psychotherapy for over twenty years. Like many of my colleagues, I consider myself to be an eclectic, rather than a purist; I have always integrated new learning into my work, and continue to do so. In the late 80's I began formal training in Marriage and Family Therapy. During the course of that training I was introduced to some of the currently popular models of Brief Therapy. I was smitten with some of the ideas that I was learning, and so continued on, taking further training in a year-long Extern Program that covered in depth the various models of Brief Therapy. That led to subsequent years of supervision, and narrowing down to what would eventually become my own style and way of working. While I was fascinated with many of the current approaches, the model that most captivated my attention was Solution Focused Brief Therapy, the stellar work of Insoo Kim Berg and Steve de Shazer. I knew that I was about to learn something that was going to forever change my way of working; I'd finally found something that I'd been searching for, for a very long time.

What came as even more of an epiphany was that what I was learning (at least in certain areas) was exactly like what I already knew! Although coming from different perspectives, Focusing Oriented Psychotherapy was so similar to Solution Oriented Therapy that I found myself continually astounded. The two models seemed the same, yet different; and where they were different, they were surprisingly compatible and complemented each other perfectly. It was so vividly apparent to me that each model gave the other what I viewed as missing pieces; frankly, I could hardly believe that no one had put them together. I committed myself, then and there, to being the one to do it. So, what follows is the result of well over a decade of practice and research (with a good share of passion thrown in!)

The term Solution Oriented Therapy comes from Bill O'Hanlon, who took the Solution Focused approach of Berg and de Shazer and added his own personal twist to it. He subsequently changed the name of his work to Possibility Therapy, but the term Solution Oriented Therapy has stayed with me. I have a real affinity for the word "oriented". It implies a direction toward…

Each of the models, Focusing Oriented and Solution Oriented Therapy, with their own unique style, pacing, and perspectives, takes the client in new directions toward healing, wellness, and solutions that work. This book is dedicated to you, the clinician. Hopefully, some of the ideas presented here will take you toward new growth and yet to be imagined possibilities.

Bala Jaison, Ph.D.

Why This? Why Now?

In this world of change, naught which comes stays, and naught which goes is lost.

Madame Swetchine

The Hopi Indians say that the difference between white people and Indians living in the desert is that during a drought white people pray for rain, while the Indians pray to adapt.

This thought appeals to me for two reasons. First, because it illustrates how very differently people view an issue, not unlike therapy, and second because I like the word *adapt.* It connotes flexibility and willingness to make change - a must in the practice of psychotherapy. We all know that no matter how much training we have had, no matter how great our teachers and mentors have been, the bottom line happens when we are sitting opposite a client in distress. It is then, in full presence, that we have to *adapt* everything we know to meet the needs of the human being sitting before us.

With the advent of Managed Care and more limited funds for long-term therapy, there has been a growing movement toward more short-term, constructive, solution-based approaches to creating change in psychotherapy, especially in the field of Brief Therapy.

Concurrently, there is some concern on the part of those who practice longer term, experientially-based psychotherapy, that the Brief Therapy approaches may be more of a band-aid and less of a cure for long-standing issues. Some Experiential clinicians feel that the Brief models, with their emphasis on brevity and their focus on finding solutions, do not take enough time to explore the affective states and experiences of the client; the therapists' skepticism, therefore, is connected to the question: *Can lasting change happen - briefly?*

The solution, so to speak, comes in the form of a both/and approach, rather than an either/or position. There is choice. There is room in the structure of a therapy session for adapting and integrating Experiential components into Brief Therapy models, and conversely, weaving Brief Solution Focused components into Experiential work. The process of integration is natural, fluid, and in fact, very effectively supports the ever-increasing trend toward a holistic mind/body approach in psychotherapy.

The purpose of this book, therefore, is to demonstrate how Experiential Therapy and Brief Therapy can work together. To illustrate, I have chosen a representative model from each orientation: Focusing Oriented Therapy from the Experiential approach and Solution Oriented Therapy from the Brief approach. I have found them so compatible that I have "married" them. This book examines the relationship between these two therapeutic partners.

Who Will Benefit From This Book?

When I was writing the original version of this book, I had always imagined that I was addressing the experienced clinician who already had a broad understanding of the diverse models of therapy. In addition, I was also wanting to make contact with the many therapy students who are currently being exposed to various models of systemic and experiential psychotherapy.

What I didn't know was that many of my clients (who empathically noticed the dark circles under my eyes after months of writing!) were also eager to read the book. To my astonishment (at least in some cases) after reading it their therapy went even better. The language of 'change' started to seep into their consciousness and conversations with me, and I found them saying things like: *"Let me see...if this wasn't happening...I wonder...what would I being doing instead?"* (Will wonders never cease!)

As my desire was to make this a totally usable book for the reader, to refer to 'at a glance', easily, without wading through words upon words (and more words!), I grappled with the issue of theory: how to present it and how much to include. So, while I have included some basic theory, I have specifically avoided making this a theoretical treatise for three reasons:

- ◊ First, the major influential figures referred to in this book have all written their own books - volumes of them. And who could write better about what they do than each of them?
- ◊ Second, because I tend to be a 'hands-on' person, I very much wanted to provide a tool-book (rather than a textbook) for therapists and counselors in clinical practice. I felt there was a need for a how-to book that could easily be picked up, read, re-read, written in, and used for quick reference in specific clinical circumstances.

◊ Finally, and maybe most importantly, I wanted to demonstrate, especially in the case examples, a method of doing psychotherapy that assiduously avoided pathologizing client issues by being solution-focused rather than problem-focused. Change can be challenging – this we know. AND change can also be approached in a creative, uplifting, and at times, in even a playful way.

This last thought was so poignantly illustrated to me in a profound workshop I attended by Steve Madigan on Anorexia and Bulimia. He asked the audience of therapists, *"How many of you have ever experienced self-esteem issues?"* Virtually everyone in the room raised their hands. Then he asked, *"How many of you have surveyed your bodies?"* Again, most hands were raised. He continued with… *"And how many of you have compared your bodies to others?"* (more hands) *"How many of you have succumbed to negative thinking?"* (That was 100%!) *"And have any of you ever been food-focused?...body-focused?...experienced fear?"* (another round of hands) *"Well"*, he said, *"anorexics just do it better!"*

I was deeply moved as he said that he wanted to look at Anorexia and Bulimia not as a "pathology of the self", but more in the context of "the interactive systems of culture".

His words summed up for me how I view the process of therapy: helping people cope better with the effects of their interactions and the culture in which they are trying to live and adapt. Have any of us as clinicians ever experienced depression? Feeling angry and negative? Fearful of the future? Feeling that we might flip out any minute? I'm assuming that the answers are a resounding "yes!" and yet, we have survived well enough to be helping others.

Hence, I offer this as a how-to book for clinicians with the intention of helping the work go better and more smoothly by demonstrating positive and constructive ways to help clients deal with the "stuff" of life - and - for any clients reading this, to hopefully show that the process of change is within your grasp.

The book will detail:

◊ The strengths and weaknesses of each model

◊ How the models are similar and different

◊ What tools from each model work best - and when

◊ How to weave the models together

◊ What to do when you don't know what to do

Most importantly, I want to highlight the specific places where the two models integrate and blend into a harmonious working relationship, because in those integration spots where the two models complement and give balance to each other, the old adage *"The whole is greater than the sum of its parts"* becomes a gratifying reality. Each model works better with the other one in it!

Helpful Guidelines

A Map for Navigating the Territory

- For the sake of brevity, I will sometimes use the word "Solution" as an abbreviation for the longer "Solution Oriented Brief Therapy"; likewise I will use the word "Focusing" to abbreviate "Focusing Oriented Therapy". I occasionally use the acronym *SOFT* to refer to the integration of the two models: Solution Oriented Focusing Therapy.

- In order to avoid awkward repetition, the following words will be used interchangeably:

  - Client/patient
  - Approach/model/work
  - Therapist/clinician/practitioner
  - Process/experience

- Avoiding confusion about the word "Focusing": In 1978, Eugene T. Gendlin wrote a book called *Focusing* which evolved directly out of his early research at the University of Chicago. It is a specific 6-step process that has been adapted for Health Care, Nursing, Mental Health, Business, Spirituality, and Creative Writing, among other disciplines. That book was never intended to be a model of therapy, but rather an integrative tool to enhance already existing models of therapy. In 1996, Gendlin wrote another book called *Focusing Oriented Psychotherapy,* which describes a model and orientation for practicing psychotherapy. It includes many of the principles outlined in the original book, *Focusing*. When I use the short form "Focusing" (unless otherwise specified) it is meant as an abbreviation for "Focusing Oriented Psychotherapy" - not the 6-step process.

- The Solution Oriented approach: there are *four interventions* that are commonly used in the practice of Brief Therapy. I will point these out at the appropriate junctures throughout this writing.

- I will point out specific INTEGRATION SPOTS to indicate the *exact places* where the two models, Focusing Oriented and Solution Oriented therapy "marry". I encourage you, the reader, to pause, take notes, and reflect upon how you can utilize the "integration spots" most naturally and effectively within the style of therapy you are currently practicing.

❖ I will highlight, as we view the models side by side, the **value** of each approach, and where each model gives the other something that would otherwise be missing. I will also underline the words Focusing and Solution before each comparison and/or contrast in order to make them easy to spot on the page for quick reference.

❖ Because I learn best by example, I have written up a number of case examples in detail. Occasionally, to make these examples more effective/efficient, I have condensed dialogues from a few different sessions into one. There are notes inserted between the client-therapist dialogues, pointing out:

◊ What the therapist is doing, and why

◊ How the session looks when the Focusing approach is used

◊ How the session looks when the Solution approach is used

◊ How the session looks when both models are woven together simultaneously

❖ For the sake of clarity, I will generally be comparing and contrasting two specific models: Focusing Oriented Therapy and Solution Oriented Therapy. However, there are several circumstances when the comparisons and contrasts refer not only to the two specific models, but apply across the board, so to speak, to all *Experiential* and *Brief* models - these times will be duly noted.

❖ Working with couples and individuals: For ease, simplicity, and clarity, some of the earlier examples demonstrate how to work with a single client, rather than a couple, even though the presenting issue is about a relationship. The purpose is to highlight and teach how the clinician can use and integrate the skills of the two models with only one person in the room, while still keeping in mind the relational and interactional components. In later case examples we will examine the complexity of integrating the two models with more than one client in the room.

❖ Being linguistically incorrect: After writing for a while, I noticed that it became cumbersome, and somewhat tiresome, to keep saying "he" and "she" and "him" and "her", when I really wanted to shorten the words to "they". Sometimes I will use "s/he" and sometimes "they"; I hope the reader will grant me some "poetic license" and excuse the occasional linguistically mismatched pronouns and verbs.

- More linguistics: To be totally correct, I should be saying: Focusing Oriented Therapy and Solution Oriented Therapy, or Focusing Oriented and Solution Oriented Therapies. The first option is occasionally too long and the second looks peculiar to me; so I will, in certain places, use the word "therapy" once, in the singular form: Focusing Oriented and Solution Oriented Therapy.

- Lastly, one of my goals in exploring the integration of Experiential and Brief Therapy is to make the work as usable as possible for the practitioner. There is a great deal of room within the models for flexibility, adaptation, and adjustment-making; my hope is that the reader will be able to tailor the approaches to fit whatever style s/he is already using. Most seasoned clinicians tend to be eclectic anyway, and are inclined to use *whatever works best* in the moment. I therefore offer the following thoughts with no *shoulds* or *have to's*. Use what fits, where it works, when it works, and most importantly - enjoy the process!

Two Schools of Thought

New ideas can be good or bad, just the same as old ones.
Franklin D. Roosevelt

The two models, Focusing Oriented Therapy and Solution Oriented Therapy, actually live under two large umbrellas. Each umbrella represents two major schools of thought: *Experiential* approaches to psychotherapy, and short-term *Brief Therapy* approaches to psychotherapy. There are numerous models of therapy under each umbrella; Focusing Oriented and Solution Oriented Therapy are two of them.

The many variations in both schools have developed over time, evolving and changing as students became practitioners, and subsequently added their own particular twists and slants. The adaptations have also been influenced by the therapists' own particular clinical experiences and the contexts in which they were practicing.

Experiential Psychotherapy

The Experiential approach evolved out of the Humanistic Psychology movement of the 60's. Some of the new buzzwords at that time were: *self-actualization*, living in the *here-and-now*, and being *present* to one's *inner journey* by *experiencing the process*. Humanistic Psychology emphasized sensitivity to feelings, internal self-discovery, exploring one's own individual essence, self-expression, communication, and congruency between one's thoughts and feelings. People talked about the *nature of being*, well summed up by Paul Tillich's famous aphorism "Being is becoming."

The work was revolutionary at the time. It represented a huge departure from traditional Psychoanalysis and Behaviorism with their emphasis on the past and early childhood experiences; the new emphasis was on, "What is going on inside of me, *right now*?" Even more significant was the importance of empowering and trusting the inner wisdom of the patient/client, another huge departure from the traditional professional-knows-all. The new Experiential models transferred the title of "expert" over to the patient.

Both movements had their pioneers, the great mentors and leading edge thinkers who influenced the new fields of psychology, and the many clinicians who followed them. Below is a sampling of some of the great figures (far too numerous to mention all of them, and my apologies to those inadvertently left out) who influenced the world of psychotherapy.

For example, under the Experiential umbrella, Fritz Perls (1969) developed *Gestalt Therapy* and the famous *empty chair* process; Virginia Satir (1967), with tremendous compassion and humor, used *family sculpting* and *therapist's use of self* to model how people related to each other - or didn't; Roberto Assagioli (1975) brought a spiritual dimension into psychotherapy by adding the perspective of the Soul; Carl Rogers (1951) developed *client-centered therapy.* Rogers emphasized the importance of the therapist-client relationship, and the attitude of the therapist toward the client which is based on respect, empathy, and "unconditional positive regard". Eugene Gendlin's (1962, 1978) work on *Experiencing* and later *Focusing* stressed the idea of congruency, and listening inside to what *the body* had to say. His patients learned how to recognize whether what they were thinking *matched* what they were feeling.

Brief Therapy

There has been a dynamic evolution in the way Brief Therapy is practiced as increasing numbers of clinicians have been introduced to the work, and adapted it to meet their specific needs.

Brief Therapy was profoundly influenced by Milton Erickson, an extraordinary and imaginative hypnotherapist from Arizona, whose attitudes towards effecting change was in its time, most unusual. It is important to recognize that behind all Brief Therapy work, including *Neuro-Linguistic Programming* (NLP) is the genius of Milton Erickson, whose approach has been suitably called "uncommon therapy." He didn't invent any therapeutic models; he simply did them. Everything after Erickson is an adaptation by other clinicians of his natural precocity.

Some of the early pioneers of Family Therapy such as Jay Haley, Don Jackson, John Weakland, and Paul Watzlawick visited and consulted with Milton Erickson. A Brief Therapy project started by Richard Fisch in 1966, within the Mental Health Research Institute at Palo Alto, had a profound effect on the development of the Brief/Strategic approach to change (Fisch, Weakland, & Segal, 1982). Two important works, *Toward a Theory of Pathological Systems*, by Haley (1967), and the other, *Pragmatics of Human Communication*, by Watzlwawick (Watzlwawick et al., 1967) made important contributions to the thinking about effecting change. In 1967, Haley joined Salvador Minuchin (1978) in Philadelphia where they conceptualized further about structure and hierarchy. The term "Strategic Therapy" was coined in Haley's (1973) influential work: *Uncommon Therapy: The Psychiatric Techniques of Milton H. Erickson.*

Particularly because of its impact on Family Therapy, interest in Brief Therapy spread rapidly in the 1970's, stimulated by Jay Haley's work and two more seminal publications from The Mental Research Institute (MRI): *Change Principles of Problem Formation and Problem Resolution* (Watzlawick *et al.,* 1974) and *Brief Therapy: Focused Problem Resolution* (Weakland *et al.*, 1974). Brief Therapy continued to grow through the 1970's and early 1980's with its emphasis on:

◊ A minimalist approach that emphasizes observable phenomenon

◊ Being pragmatic in effecting change

◊ The theory that problems are produced and maintained by repetitive behavioral sequences, both personal and interpersonal

Brief Therapy evolved from being *problem* and *present* oriented, to *solution* and *future* oriented with the breakthrough work of Steve de Shazer (1985) *Keys to Solution in Brief Therapy* and *Family Preservation: A Brief Workbook*, by Insoo Kim Berg (1991) at the Brief Therapy Institute, in Wisconsin, which they called "Solution Focused Brief Therapy".

Berg and de Shazer popularized the deceivingly simple application of their model through the late 1980's and 1990's. While Solution Focused Brief Therapy has now been adapted world wide, it was initially intended to address a variety of disorders and emergency situations: the borderline criminal element, alcoholics, welfare recipients, and extremely dysfunctional and/or abusive families. The work has proven to be highly effective in terms of making positive changes rapidly.

William O'Hanlon, a colleague of Berg and de Shazer, added his own particular twist to the Solution Focused Brief Therapy model; he was influenced by both Carl Rogers in the *experiential client-centered* approach, as well as by Ericksonian hypnotherapy. He called his adaptation *Solution Oriented Brief Therapy*, and wrote his own breakthrough work, *In Search of Solutions: A New Direction in Psychotherapy* (O'Hanlon & Weiner-Davis, 1989). His work evolved further over time into what O'Hanlon (1997) called *Possibility Therapy* - his way of continually broadening the focus of the work into other realms; for example, by incorporating spiritual components.

The field of Brief Therapy continues to expand, and as it does, so do the variations and new possibilities. Increasingly, working with a solution orientation is becoming more viable, more realistic, and easier to integrate for clinicians practicing longer term, in-depth therapy.

The Solution Approach

Human motivation is much more complicated than what is the right or wrong thing to do.

Insoo Kim Berg

To the untrained eye, a Solution Oriented Therapy interview can look too simple to be true. To the trained eye of the depth-oriented Experiential therapist, it can look gimmicky. It is neither. The approach was derived from many years of studying how clients get stuck in patterns of behavior, and what needs to happen to move toward radical change. The beauty of the model's simplicity is in its emphasis on how to effect change respectfully and effectively. Therefore, it might be helpful here to outline some of the underlying assumptions taken from *Becoming Solution-Focused in Brief Therapy,* by John Walter and Jane Peller (1992):

1. Identifying the *positive*, the *solution*, and the *future*, facilitates change in the desired direction. "Solution-oriented talk" vs. "problem-oriented talk.

2. There are exceptions to *every* problem. By finding them, the therapist and client can think in terms of creating change, which can be used to build solutions.

3. Change is occurring all the time.

4. Small changes lead to bigger changes.

5. Clients are always cooperating. They are showing us how they think changes take place. As we understand their thinking and act accordingly, cooperation is inevitable.

6. Meaning and Experience are interactionally constructed. Meaning is the world, or medium, in which we live. We inform meaning onto our experience, and it is our experience at the same time. Meaning is not imposed from without or determined from outside ourselves. We inform our world through interaction.

7. People have all they need to solve their problems.

8. Actions and descriptions are circular. A change in meaning (a reframe) can change how the client informs further events, and what the client consequently does behaviorally.

9. The meaning of the message is what the client responds to; for example, meaning vs. intent. If it's not working, *do something different.*

10. The client is the expert regarding the readiness for change.

11. Any change in how clients describe a goal (solution) and/or what they do, affects future interactions with all others involved. So, for example, couples counseling with only one spouse can have an impact on the whole marital system.

12. The members of a treatment group are those who share the feeling that there is a goal, and state their desire to do something about making it happen. Goals need to be achievable. A solution-constructed model of therapy cuts across labeling, diagnoses, and the distinction of individual and family therapy.

Note to experiential therapists: It is easy to read these twelve points, and think, "Yes, that sounds good"...or..."reasonable". I encourage experientially oriented practitioners to take the time to reflect on each of these points in order to integrate them philosophically and internally, with the experiential perspective; they are quite profound.

The Focusing Approach

Let us watch well our beginnings, and results will manage themselves.

Alexander Clarke

Eugene T. Gendlin, Ph.D. was both a student, and later a colleague, of Carl Rogers. He developed, and is the author of *Focusing* (Gendlin, 1978), an exquisitely simple, yet profound process of *listening inside* oneself to what he has termed the "felt-sense" or "bodily felt-sense" of one's experience.

During the 1960's, Gendlin, a professor at the University of Chicago, conducted a fascinating and revealing research project along with his colleagues. What they wanted to know was:

- ◊ Why doesn't psychotherapy succeed more often?
- ◊ Does psychotherapy really make a lasting difference in people's lives, or not?
- ◊ When it does succeed - Why?
- ◊ Is it something the therapist is doing?
- ◊ Is it something the client is doing?
- ◊ What needs to happen to make therapy more successful more often?

They studied thousands of hours of therapist-patient interactions, tape recording various styles of psychotherapy from the classical approaches to the newer Experiential models.

To their astonishment they discovered that they could tell within the first two sessions - and sometimes within the first few minutes! - which clients would have a successful therapy experience, and which ones would not.

(What an astounding responsibility to know that someone is embarking on months of therapy, which will have very little effect. But that was not the project. The project was to determine what worked and what didn't - and why?)

After listening to and documenting hundreds of hours of audiotapes, they had some startling revelations:

◊ The success of any particular therapy session had to do more with the client than the therapist.

◊ The style of therapy being employed was not significant to the outcome of the session, nor was the content of what the client presented.

◊ Change actually happened through *something* the clients were doing *internally* and *naturally, inside* of themselves (often without awareness).

◊ What these clients were doing that produced change, whether it was conscious or not, was:

a) so obvious, that it could be spotted immediately;
b) easily explained, and could be taught to both students and colleagues.

And what was this *thing* that these clients were doing?

First, when they spoke or attempted to express their issues they were:

- speaking *from* themselves rather than talking about themselves
- they were *listening to* themselves rather than *talking at* themselves

Said another way, it's the difference between:
Thinking that *you know* - vs. - *knowing* that *you know*.

This *felt-knowing* came to be known as *Focusing*: the ability to *listen inside* to the *felt-sense* of one's *direct experience*.

The felt-sense is the body's *holistically registered experience* of a situation or issue. More explicitly, it is the *body's sense* of a particular problem or issue, rather than the mind's interpretation of the same thing. The felt-sense is always directly connected to issues and feelings in an individual's life, and has a definite quality that "fits", "matches", or "resonates" with the feelings one has about the issue. The *felt-sense is not an emotion*. It is the holistic sense of the totality of the problem or issue – what Gendlin often refers to as "*the whole thing*".

One of the premises behind Focusing is based on the theory that everything we experience from the moment of birth is registered in the body in a cellular way, whether or not we consciously remember it. By paying attention to, and "keeping company" with the felt-sense of our experience, and by listening attentively to what this felt-sense has to say, it is possible to get new and valuable information that is *more* than one can receive from the cognitive mind alone.

Over time Gendlin realized that the Focusing process could be developed into a teaching model, not only for psychology students, but also for the clients themselves.

Consider, for a moment, what a radical idea that was: to teach clients how to be better clients! Gendlin very astutely points out that "psychotherapy as usually practiced doesn't show patients how to *do* psychotherapy." They are *in* the experience with the therapist, but often have no idea *how* they actually arrive at an insight or shift. In other words, psychotherapy may not be an area where "practice makes perfect". In fact, just the reverse may be true: *if clients have to keep coming and coming ad infinitum, perhaps change is not happening!*

Focusing 101: How To...

Let me start off with a bit of an oxymoron or paradox:

Focusing is being taught all over the world - AND - it is almost impossible to teach Focusing!

Some elaboration...yes, Focusing is being taught (and taught really well!) by many highly skilled and well-trained people. This process has been integrated into a number of modalities beyond therapy (e.g. business, education, the arts, medicine, etc.) And/also in certain respects it is actually difficult and challenging to teach. Why? Because the process is *experiential;* it takes place in the here-and-now, in a person's direct experience in-the-moment. Thus, as soon as you use words to talk *about* it, you are no longer *in* it!

Having said that, Focusing is obviously teachable, and those of us teaching it have worked hard to find the best ways to communicate *what* Focusing *is*...

The following is my attempt to communicate *what* Focusing *is*...to make the process more understandable, not only on a cognitive level, but a visceral one as well. The importance of this visceral knowing will be evident later, when the concepts of Solution Oriented (Brief) Therapy are brought into the mix. What I am wanting is for the reader and I to be on the "same (*felt*) page", in order to facilitate the smooth integration of these two styles of therapy (Brief and Experiential) while always keeping the *integrity of Focusing intact.*

Hence, albeit unusual, the following pages offer a *visual/experiential* crash-course in Focusing, making it possible for the readers of this book to visually 'see' the same thing. Let's start first with a definition of Focusing:

Focusing is...

Paying attention inside...to something that is not yet clear, but definitely *felt* or *experienced* by the body, and distinctly connected to something in our lives – AND – by paying attention, and *staying with* the unclear *bodily felt-sense* (of an issue, situation, feeling or person), movement or steps forward will occur that produce *change* - not necessarily of the issue or problem - but in our *relationship* to "it", creating a feeling of relief, called a *felt-shift* (or the *'ah ha' experience*).

Paying Attention

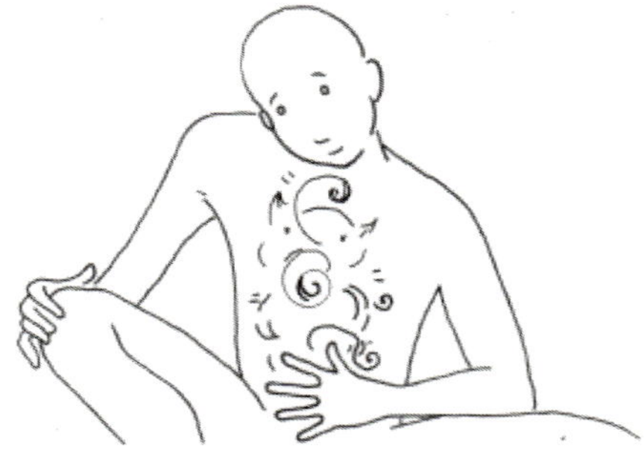

The first step of Focusing involves bringing awareness *into the body.* In Focusing we say that "in the body" means the area between the throat, chest, stomach, and lower abdomen. Why? Because this is the general area where *feelings reside.* Consider for a moment the expressions that we use to describe feelings (in that center area of the body): *I had a lump in my throat...so choked up with emotion; My stomach was in knots from the upset; My heart was pounding out of my chest...*

So, we begin the Focusing experience by *paying attention inside:* getting quiet, gently bringing attention into the body, and scanning the area between the throat, chest, stomach, and lower abdomen. Then we just watch, and wait…and begin *noticing...*this is beginning of the process of *Focusing...*

Felt-Sense: The Body's Experience

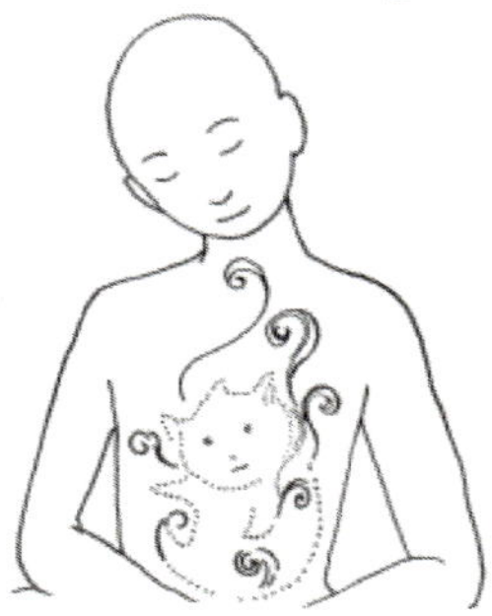

As we sit with: What all is *'there' (inside)... 'something'* begins to form, to take shape…a kind of 'sense about'… *What is all this connected to in my life, right now...?*

This forming *inner-understanding* or *felt-knowing* is called the "felt-sense". It is the *body's experience* of a situation or feeling. Said another way, if you could take your mind and place it into your body (the *body's mind* or the bodily 'take' on a situation) this would be a felt-sense. The formation of a felt-sense takes a little while to develop - about 30 seconds - which is why we need to just 'sit with it'. As we allow *what's inside* to grow, the inner sense begins to *take shape*…and becomes a fully developed…

Felt-Sense

In Focusing, we say that a felt-sense has a *life* of its own (separate from our cognitive thoughts). A felt-sense is *alive*, has its own *rhythms*, its own *frequency*, its own *unique quality*, directly connected to an issue, situation, person, place or thing (in our lives).

A felt-sense can be joyful, such as…*all about that wonderful feeling*… and the practice of Focusing is applicable to anything and everything that is worth spending some time with or developing further, such as creative projects or one's *sensed* next steps of growth, development, or budding edges…OR…

A Felt Sense Can Be...

A felt-sense can be more troubling: a sinking feeling, knotted up, resistant, or overwhelmed. There are many different kinds of *felt-senses*, each *uniquely connected* to our *distinctive feelings* about *something*. It is very common for a felt-sense to have no real words (in proper language) to describe its essence. Felt-sense words tend to be more amorphous: yukky, ughhhh, icky, blah…these can all be perfect words (or *inner* representations) to exactly describe a felt-sense.

It is also important to understand that the felt-sense is 'more' than an emotion; it is wider and more inclusive. Each *felt-sense* contains (whether it is known, or still developing in awareness) the *whole* of the issue – *all of it.* An emotion is smaller and sharper than a felt-sense. For example, we might say: *"I feel bad"* and with it a gnawing feeling in the stomach. But…when we sit with the felt-sense of "What is this 'bad' connected to in my life?" a 'more' will come: *I don't feel cared for or valued…hummm, it's something like that…I feel like…nothing…yes, that's it! I feel like 'nothing'…the felt-sense of all this 'bad' is like an empty hole with nothing in it! – YES – THAT'S what IT is…!!"*

Without paying attention inside, and sitting with the vague, unclear feelings, it would be impossible to know that the initial "bad" is actually held in the body as an "empty hole with nothing in it" – which *exactly* describes the felt-sense.

The Focusing Attitude

Having an issue or problem is difficult enough. Learning how to *be with* an issue or problem is even more complex, especially if there is a critical element: *"I hate myself"; "I really blew it this time"; "I can never win"*. So imagine that something is bothering you, and you're waiting patiently to get in to see a therapist. The therapist is always kind, empathic, understanding, and above all listens to you, with both care and concern. You feel safe to tell this therapist anything, and you know that he or she will listen to you with non-judgment and non-blame, simply permitting or allowing whatever you say to be held safely, with no repercussions for having said it. THIS is the *Focusing Attitude,* and it is easier said than done – especially if you don't like how you are feeling.

So when we begin the Focusing process, the first thing we do (acting like the therapist, or wise person - *to ourselves*) is say: *HELLO (in there)* and invite whatever wishes to speak to do so: with kindness, gentleness, and the same attitude you would have with a best friend: *You can tell me anything, and I'm here for you*. Even if we don't like *'what comes'* (the *part* that is troublesome, resistant, whining, scared, etc.) we greet *it* (the felt-sense) with an *attitude* of ever-present respect (exactly as we would with a client or really good friend).

What Gets In The Way Of Focusing

Too Close

A *Too Close* process means feeling overwhelmed, over-taken, over-burdened. The feeling becomes so big, so intense, so intrusive, consuming so much space and time, that we experience the feeling as 'bigger' than we are – so big, in fact, that we can't find (or lose) our 'I' or 'Self'. (Have you ever said: "I am *'beside'* myself" or "The problem is so huge that there's no *'me'* left.")

Too Distant

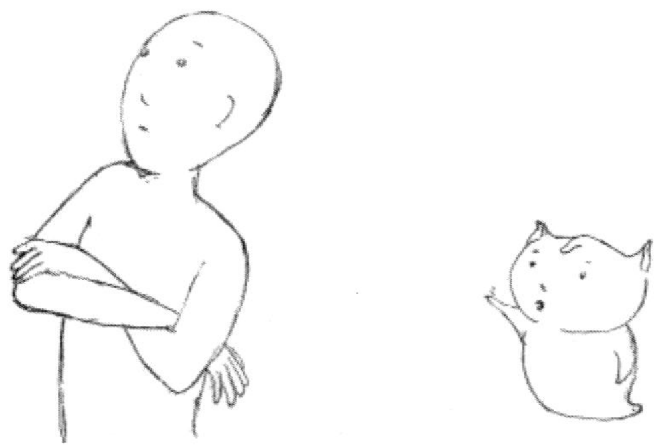

A *Too Distant* process happens for many reasons: Sometimes we just wish it would *go away*, so we try to ignore or minimize the feelings, hoping we won't have to deal with them. Sometimes, a memory or perhaps a trauma is so painful that we dissociate from the felt-sense, so as not to re-live the pain. Sometimes a person is cut-off or "out of touch" with experiencing feelings. The bottom line is that a 'Too Distant process' means that we are disconnected from the feeling state.

Right Relationship

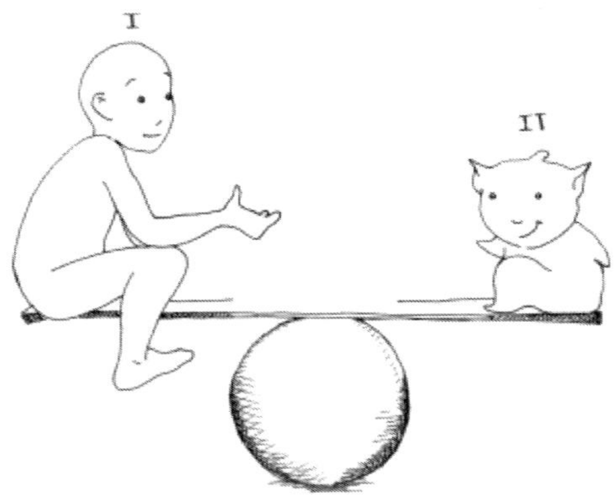

In order for Focusing to work at its best, we need to be in what we call a *right relationship with our felt-sense* (or issue, or concern or whatever we are working with). What does that mean? It means *just the right distance* (which varies with each individual felt-sense of an issue): Close enough to get a *'feel'* for the issue, but not so close as to get overwhelmed.

In Focusing, this is what is referred to as the "I/It Relationship". "I" refers to the Self, the Adult, the one who has wisdom - who *knows*. "It" refers to the issue or problem, or the "part" that feels a certain way (sad, for example). Notice the difference between these two phrasings: "I AM sad." vs. "There's a *part of me* that feels very sad, right now." In the first example, the implication is that *all of me* is sad – that's who "I AM". In the second example, by creating or conceptualizing that there is a *part* that carries the sadness, there is still an "I" who remains all OK and able to cope with and nurture the not-OK-part.

It is extremely helpful to use imagery to find exactly the right 'way' to be in relationship to an issue. Often times this entails finding a right 'place' to put the issue: *"I will sit in a rowboat, and leave the issue on the shore, then I can decide how close to the shore feels comfortable for me to be"* - or - *"The felt-sense of this issue is fragile - it needs comfort. I'll put it right here on the couch next to me, and put my arm around it."* - or - *"I'm not ready to work on this today. I'll put it over there on my desk so I can keep an eye on it."* It is important to take as much time as necessary to establish *just* the *right relationship* with the felt-sense of an issue, feeling, or situation.

Congruency

Sometimes we are really in sync with ourselves, that is, the *mind says* something like: *"I really need to take some time to clean my desk and file my papers."* And the *body,* or *bodily felt-sense,* in total agreement says: *"That's a great idea – let's do it!"* In Focusing this is called a *'fit'* or a *'match'*.

Non-match

A non-match or lack of congruency happens when we notice that what we *think* and what we *feel* do not agree. This time, we say: *"Let's clean up the desk",* and the felt-sense becomes resistant and says: *"I don't want to"* - or goes into avoidance or procrastination. This is where we begin to *sit with*…"What is this really *all about*…?" and with the Focusing Attitude (of openness and non-judgment), we invite the felt-sense to speak and tell us its story: "So…there's *something there*, that doesn't want to…*I'm listening…tell me all about it…"*

Listening

The ability to listen inside, and hear openly and freshly what the felt-sense is "carrying around" (as if you've never heard it before) is the crux of being able to fully experience Focusing. It is a process of listening, with *total openness and acceptance*, to *whatever inside* wants to speak – again, with no blame, judgment, criticism or preconceived notions.

And – it takes a little time: Sometimes because we feel anxious or concerned about what we will hear; sometimes because it is difficult to face an uncomfortable issue or situation; and sometimes because we just don't know what will emerge (again, the importance of inner safety).

So, we get very quiet inside, *inviting* the felt-sense *to speak, share, tell its story*, and we *listen: deeply and empathically,* with *care* and *concern.*

Asking

In Focusing, there are *gentle, open-ended questions* that we learn to ask which encourage and invite the felt-sense to speak, unfold, expand, and eventually *shift* to a better-feeling and more congruent inner place. The questions that we pose are generally very wide and invitational:

- *What is this really about for me...?*
- *What is making this ___(e.g. "yukky") feeling...?*
- *What is it...that makes me feel this way...?*
- *What is my sense of the whole thing...?*

Then there are questions that point to: What's wrong:

- *What is really the worst of this...?*
- *What's my sense about the real crux of this...?*
- *What is it that feels so...?* (fill in *felt* word: *queasy, uneasy, sinking*, etc.)
- *What's between me and feeling really good, right now...?*

And there are questions that point to: What would be right:

- *What does this (felt-sense) need...?*
- *What would feel like a step toward fresh air...?*
- *What feels like a bit of relief...?*
- *If this whole thing* (issue) *had a voice and could speak to me...what would it want me to know...*

Felt-Shift

A *felt-shift*, when it occurs, is the *'ah ha' experience,* where *our relationship* to the issue *changes* or *shifts.* The issue may still be there, unresolved, but how we *hold* or *carry* the issue inside feels dramatically different e.g., *I'm still disappointed that I can't go because I got the flu, but now I feel more at peace with it – instead of devastated – about it.*

In Focusing we sometimes call this *'fresh air'*, *'relief'*, or finding the *'life-forward energy'*. The issue may not be totally resolved, but our *relationship with "it"* has changed.

Before we make closure from a Focusing experience, we take some extra time to *welcome*, *receive*, and say an *inner 'thank you'* for what came inside. This is a very respectful and gentle moment, where we appreciate the process of *processing.* This is also a time to: *internally mark the spot*, in case we would like to come back to it again, at a later time.

The Critic

(The 'part' you DON'T want to meet!)

And the biggest obstacle to Focusing.

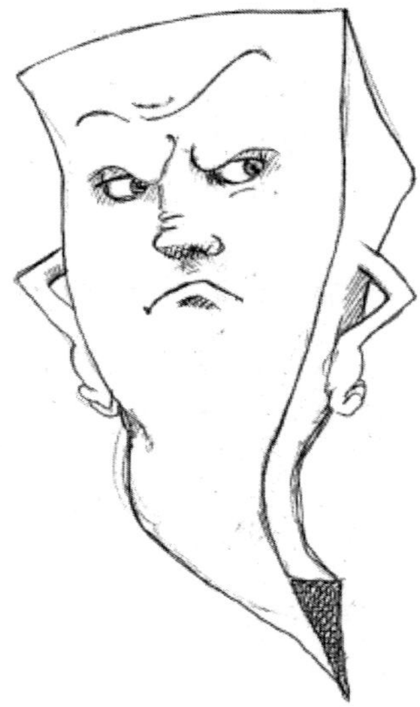

Just as we get a felt-sense of what *feels right*, we want to learn to recognize the felt-sense of what *feels wrong*, bad, harmful, destructive, and *not OK* inside.

The Critic is a compilation of critical 'voices' and negative messages that have been *internalized* from early childhood to the present. The words of these collective 'others' have been taken into our bodies as 'true', and become distorted into very painful and unhappy-making messages.

The Critic is first and foremost a name-caller

- ABUSIVE
- BLAMING
- IMPATIENT
- JUDGING

The Critic gives the impression that it is here to help you. A useful analogy would be to imagine an adult spanking a child, all the while saying *"I'm just doing this for your own good"*.

The truth is that there are more positive and constructive ways to learn - and engaging in a dialogue with the Critic is not one of them!

Me, Myself, and I...

When the Critic wedges its way in between the authentic Self and the (often vulnerable) felt-sense, the wisdom of the Self is *cut-off* or *separated* from its natural holistic connection to its own inner knowing. The Critic becomes the "I" in relationship to the felt-sense. Its messages are harsh, and its attitude is abusive.

Establishing a Right Connection

And so, in Focusing we make every effort to *stay connected* with the felt-sense of our experience. We listen, we maintain an attitude of caring, attempting to learn and grow in ways that are positive, constructive, and ever respectful.

This is the beginning of using the Focusing process to find the steps forward to healing and wellness...

How the Approaches are Similar and Compatible

Tell me with whom thou art found, and I will tell thee who thou art.

Goethe

The bridging word that joins Focusing Oriented Therapy with Solution Oriented Therapy is "oriented" which implies *leaning toward, in the direction of, so inclined* (Webster, 1981). Both of these models are *oriented* in a very similar direction: Changing how the client *views* (Solution language) or *carries inside* (Focusing language) the problem. Both models might be characterized as *wellness* work (versus paying attention to, or emphasizing *pathology*). Thus, each model concerns itself with what will be creative, life enhancing, and positive for the client. Focusing often calls it finding "fresh air". The parallel in the Solution model is asking the client about what will be "helpful" (in finding relief from the problem). In Focusing we look for *what feels right,* in the Solution model for *what works*.

Gendlin frequently uses the analogy of an elevator. He talks about putting one's attention *in the body*, again in the area spanning the throat, chest, stomach, and lower abdomen, and then traveling down the elevator, or "going downstairs" to the floor, or level, where the Focusing experience takes place.

Staying with this analogy, we might say that Solution Oriented Therapy (and in fact, all Brief Therapy) takes place on a different floor than Focusing Oriented Therapy (and all Experiential approaches). To better understand the Solution Oriented model (in contrast to the Focusing Oriented model) it is helpful to think in terms of taking the elevator a bit *higher* up to a more *cognitive* level. Hence, integrating the Focusing and Solution models might be viewed as heading in the *same direction,* but on *different floors.*

Another way to view the two models is to imagine them functioning on *parallel planes*, or in *parallel universes*. The important point is that both models are headed in a similar, compatible, and positive direction.

Philosophy and Attitude

There is one person that is wiser than anybody, and that is everybody.
Alexander Talleyrand-Perigord

Philosophically, there is a similarity between the Focusing Oriented and Solution Oriented models. Embedded in the core of each approach is a deep belief that the client has enormous resources, strengths, natural competencies, and life experience. The job of the clinician is to draw forth from the client what is *already there*. When the therapist validates what the client already intuitively knows, and communicates to the client through: listening responses, facial expressions, body language, and "attitude", the client begins to experience the feeling that what s/he has to say is worthwhile and of value. Through the therapist's ongoing encouragement and support, clients gradually learn how to access their own innate capabilities. Both models share the view that the client already has the *solution* inside; Focusing calls this *bodily-felt wisdom*.

Also common to both the Solution and Focusing approaches is a manner of being with clients that models the utmost respect: positive, receptive, non-judgmental, and most importantly, deeply acknowledging of the client as the expert in his or her own process of development.

The Focusing Oriented therapist puts far more emphasis, however, on the manner in which the therapist relates to the client - a key factor toward healing in this model; hence Gendlin's term, the "Focusing Attitude" has particular meaning for the Focusing Oriented therapist. The Focusing approach tends to stress the client's sense of safety, first externally in relationship to the therapist, and eventually to others; then internally, meaning how clients relate inwardly and respectfully to themselves. Clients are taught how to "greet whatever comes inside" with this attitude of friendliness and welcoming, or at least "allowing and permitting" whatever wants to speak to do so, without criticism, judgment, or blame. The therapist consistently affirms and empowers the client by being fully present, and listening with empathic support and encouragement.

The Solution Oriented therapist does not speak directly with the client about "attitude", however the fundamental belief in the client's inherent expertise is quite naturally modeled through an attitude of ongoing respect. Further, by asking clients questions that are worded to evoke a feeling of competence in the client, the attitude of respect is already implied.

Orientation Toward the Positive

It will always do to change for the better.

J. Thomson

Both models operate on the *assumption* that the innate wisdom of the client is ready and waiting to be tapped. The Solution model does this by looking for "what's right"; the Focusing model by looking for "pro-life energy", "fresh air", and "the OK place inside".

Focusing

A major foundational piece underlying the philosophy of the Focusing Oriented approach is the concept of *essential wholeness*. Gendlin states that we are "all already OK". We are all already whole, well, and perfect in essence, but then "things come" that "stand in the way" of us and experiencing that essential wholeness. When these obstacles that "stand in the way" present themselves, the therapist looks for ways to tap into any possibilities that might lead to some positive forward movement, "fresh air" or "pro-life energy".

For example, if the client says, *"I'm depressed",* instead of the clinician reflecting back, *"It sounds like you are depressed",* the Focusing Oriented therapist says, "So, there's *a part* of you that is feeling depressed, right now."

Or, the therapist, in response to *"I'm depressed"* might say: *"Can you just take a minute here...to see if there's any part of you...even a small part...that isn't depressed, right now."*

I would ask the reader here to stop for a moment and *sense* the difference between "*I am* depressed" (or angry or upset) and "there's *a part* of me that feels that (negative) way". Implicit in pointing to the *part* that feels depressed is the assumption that there is some part that *doesn't* feel depressed. So, in the Focusing Oriented approach, even if a client says s/he is 90% depressed, the clinician will take the time to "make room" for the 10% that is "all OK", before embarking upon the problem.

Solution

The Solution Oriented approach guides the client to exactly the same positive place by finding the *Exception to the Problem.* This intervention was developed by Insoo Kim Berg and Steve de Shazer of the Brief Family Therapy Center in Milwaukee.

1st INTERVENTION ⬣ *Exception to the Problem*

The therapist looks for exceptions to the problem by posing questions that imply and encourage the client to explore those times when the problem was less - or not at all. The *exception questions* tend to fall into two categories: finding exceptions in the past which highlight when the client or situation was better, and finding exceptions in the present which deal with how the client is managing to cope, right now. The latter are called "coping questions".

Past exceptions:

◊ *When was the last time things were better?* (or if the situation is more critical)...*a little bit better?*

- *What was happening then...that seemed different for you, than now?*
- *What did you notice...about those times...?*
- *Do you remember what were you doing differently then?*

◊ When was the last time you felt you were successful at handling the problem?

- *What were you doing then that was different?*
- *How do you imagine it will be when it is right...or better?*

Present exceptions: (coping questions)

◊ *Given the incredible stress you've been under, I can't help wondering how you've managed so well up to now?*

or

◊ *How did you manage to even get out of bed to come here today?*

The point: always looking for what is right, the tiny exception, the small ray of light that the therapist and client(s) can build upon together. These *exceptions* create a sense of hopefulness and expectation for clients as they begin to envision a more positive and viable future.

The Solution Picture

Another way that the Solution model points to the positive is by co-constructing with clients what Berg and DeShazer refer to as "The Solution Picture": having the client imagine in detail, based on their *personal meaning*, how it will look when it is *right*, (or in Focusing parlance) *all OK*.

Over time, the picture is developed, changed, modified, and adapted into a vision of the future that is hopeful, and more important, *possible* for the client to achieve.

If negatives come up in the process of creating the Solution Picture, they are *reframed* by the therapist who offers (or reflects) an alternative label to a client's behavior. Hence, the presenting issue or problem takes on a slightly different and more positive meaning and connotation making it easier for the client to effect therapeutic change. For Example:

- ◊ The over-functioning parent is really "concerned".
- ◊ The procrastinator just wants to "do it right".
- ◊ The stingy person wants to make sure they can "meet their needs".
- ◊ The controller has very "high standards" of quality.

Value: The careful construction of the Solution Picture, using more positive (reframed) words and concepts (with which the client feels resonant) assists him/her in seeing and staying connected with the idea of *new visions* and *new possibilities*.

Focusing

The Focusing approach to finding the Solution Picture starts with the I/it relationship, i.e., finding a new relationship to "it".

Keep in mind that:

"I" refers to the whole and healthy core being that is well and all OK.

"It" refers to two possible things:

◊ The *issue*, which is "standing in the way" of experiencing our essential wholeness.

◊ The *part* that carries the issue, and consequently feels separate or split off, from the "I".

Gendlin, in his attempt to help clients experience the distinction between "I" and "it", developed a specific tool called "Clearing A Space" (which is actually the first step of the original 6-step Focusing model). It is a process in which clients learn to:

◊ Get some distance from the problem or issue in order to view *it* with a different perspective (as in backing up from a very large painting in order to take in the whole picture).

◊ Form a "right relationship" or "right distance" with the issue in order to emphasize: "I am *not* the issue; I *have* the issue."

◊ Sort, itemize, and prioritize the various issues: e.g., *All about my work... All about my relationship... All about the sad feelings...* and so on. The client can then begin to experience the issues differently: *What's big... What's not-so-big after all... What needs attention right now...* and *What can wait...*

Value: taking the time to experience the Self in its wholeness, separate from the *stuff* that clutters the internal space.

The Focusing Oriented therapist may or may not take the time to go through the full process of "Clearing A Space" during a session. However, within the course of the hour, if the client's issue feels overwhelming or "too close", the therapist may make some gentle suggestions, such as asking the client if he or she can "back up from it a little", or put it somewhere "at a distance", so that the "I" can breathe/exist - separate from the issue.

Conversely, if the client is experiencing a "too distant" process and feeling disconnected from... or having difficulty connecting to... what s/he is talking about, the therapist will work with the client to find a safe or more manageable way to "bring it in" - just close enough to "touch it around the edges", but not so close that it becomes overwhelming.

INTEGRATION SPOT

Even if Brief Therapy is the orientation of choice, consider taking a moment to help clients better prepare for the therapy hour. Often they are hurrying in at the last moment, feeling stressed, and not quite in sync with what they are about to do.

It is very effective to ask them to:

Take a minute to close their eyes, if they are comfortable doing that. If they are not (or find closing their eyes strange in some way, or too cut off or isolated), simply let them know that just for this moment, it is *not necessary to relate to you* (the therapist). They are welcome to close their eyes, or stare out the window, or gaze into space. The clinician then continues:

> *Take a few deep breaths...and allow yourself to wind down…and just be here...*

Then ask the client to reflect upon any or all of the following:

> *How am I doing, right now...?*
> *What is important for me today...?*
> *Is there anything in my life that feels like it needs attention, right now...?*
> *How do I want to use the next hour...?*

Example:

The client has just reflected upon one of the above questions, for instance, *How am I doing, right now?* and responds with irritation and in a somewhat explosive manner:

CLIENT: How am I doing? You want to know how I'm doing? I feel like crap…is how I feel!

THERAPIST (slowly): So is that where we want to start?…All about...feeling like crap?

CLIENT: Yeah, but…there's also a whole issue about my daughter.

THERAPIST OK...So there's a lot going on today…Can you just take a moment to see…when you say to yourself, *All about…I feel like crap*…and *All about… the issue with my daughter*…where you sense is the right place for us to start today...

CLIENT: OK...I want to talk about my daughter…that's part of why I feel like crap anyway!

This may seem like a small point, but the client is now fully focused and present to the issue. He came in unfocused and vaguely connected to "I feel like crap." He is now tuned-in to "all about my daughter" and ready to go to work on it.

INTEGRATION: Start a Brief Therapy session with an *experiential moment* to slow down; it will help the client become more present and attentive to the work at hand - and the session will go better!

How the Approaches are Different

"Where there is no difference, there is only indifference."
Louis Nizar

There are some fundamental differences, both theoretically and conceptually, between the long-term and short-term approaches to therapy. The differences are especially evident in a) how each approach views the therapeutic process and its purpose; b) the underlying assumptions and beliefs about how clients change; and c) the role of the therapist is in helping clients make change. The differences may at first seem quite far apart, however I believe the disparities can (and should) be bridged.

There are differences in how Brief and Experiential clinicians view the questions:

◊ What is the definition of success in therapy?

◊ When is the therapy process finished? Who decides, the therapist or the client?

◊ What are the time constraints?

To begin, I would like to tie together the first question: *What is the definition of success in therapy?* with the last question: *What are the time constraints?* because I believe they have a direct bearing on each other.

Brief Therapy

Theories are ideas that develop out of experience, observation and practice. The ideas behind the Brief and short-term approaches to therapy, and the way therapy is practiced, have certainly been influenced by time parameters and deadlines (as a backdrop) for determining how long the therapy process would/should take. Through observation and experience with clients, the pioneers of the short-term approach were clear that addressing directly: *What do you see as the problem? How will it be when it is no longer a problem? How can we help you get there?* was a viable and efficient way to meet the practical needs of clients, especially in the areas of crisis intervention and/or limited funds for therapy. So, with the idea of time constraints as a consideration: *What is the definition of success in therapy?*

To measure the success of a therapy experience we need to understand, *What is the goal?* For the Brief therapist the major goal is to resolve the presenting problem. While there are numerous "techniques" to enhance the practice of Brief Therapy, the orientation toward being brief has more to do with a definite way of thinking about the fundamentals of change and how to help clients construct solutions, based on their stated goals that will help them make those changes. One of the most basic assumptions underlying the Brief approach is the orientation toward the positive and the assumption that change is always possible. Clients are encouraged to notice what is working and how they can do more of what works. The orientation toward what is right and possible keeps the process focused in the future (rather than dwelling on the possible or probable causes of the problem). The Brief therapist is working with the client on developing strategies that will lead to what the client wants, and the steps that will help them reach their stated goals.

So, with the idea of time constraints as a backdrop, *What is the definition of success in therapy?*

Here are some of the indicators that might signal success in Brief therapy:

- ◊ Has the problem been solved, or is it occurring less frequently?
- ◊ Have the problematic behavioral patterns of the client(s) changed through the process of therapy?
- ◊ Is the client doing more positive and constructive things/behaviors?
- ◊ How does the client see his/her life differently when their worldview includes the new positive changes and possibilities?
- ◊ Does the client seem more positive and satisfied?
- ◊ Is the client noticing an increased sense of competence and feeling more hopeful about his/her future?
- ◊ Does the client notice how his/her changes affect relationships with other significant people in his/her life?

The standard for judging the success of therapy is directly connected to whether the therapist and client can respond to the above questions with a "Yes". If the client feels better and is behaving differently, if the problematic behaviors are less frequent and therefore having a less negative impact on others, then the Brief clinician considers therapy a success, at least for the time being.

Termination does not preclude the client from returning at some further point for future issues. The therapist lets clients know that they are welcome to return if they are experiencing difficulties, and that returning at a later date is not an indication of failure, but rather an opportunity to experience more change.

Experiential Therapy

One of the major differences between the short-term and long-term approaches is that the theories and concepts underlying the Experiential models were not developed within a framework of being time-bound. With time as a non-issue, therapists were free to concentrate on the "whole person". Rather than focusing on the problem or the solution, the Experiential pioneers concentrated on *What is psychological wholeness and well-being? What impedes the development of wholeness? How can the therapist help the client to move into full presentness in life?*

The answers to these questions were developed with clients through experiential processing. The therapist emphasized the importance of feelings and emotions which were generally expressed by the client in the present during the session; time was made available to explore old internalized issues that might negatively condition the present such as past disappointments, rejection, fears, defenses, and self-esteem issues. The theory was that by taking the time to explore these latent feelings, the client would have a better understanding and appreciation of the present. The underlying assumption was (and is) that change will happen by exploring congruence between inner experience and outer behavior. Clients were therefore encouraged to spend time developing more awareness around issues such as personal fulfillment, individuality, and untapped inner potential with a goal toward optimum psychological growth.

Hence, in the case of long-term Experiential therapy, with the idea that time is not a major restriction, *What is the definition of success in therapy?* and *What is the goal?*

For the Experiential therapist, the major goal is to help the client experience whatever the obstacles to change are, and to help the client re-experience (freshly) what feels like new growth - a new right way, in the present; the Experiential perspective is that when the client can directly experience congruence, change happens naturally.

It should be noted that clinicians who are drawn to Experiential approaches do their work with some element of faith: faith in the process, faith in the client's ability to find his/her own unique right directions, faith that most people have within them an intrinsic wholeness that may have gotten lost or sidetracked, but that can be re-accessed in therapy with time and patience.

Some of the indicators that signal success in Experiential therapy:

- ◊ Is the client happier and more fulfilled?
- ◊ Is the client's behavior more congruent with how they are actually feeling?
- ◊ Is the client more able to communicate inwardly and outwardly?
- ◊ Does the client seem to have more insight and awareness of his/her behavioral patterns, both inner and outer?
- ◊ Does the client seem more energized and positive?
- ◊ How does the client feel differently about the new positive changes?
- ◊ Is the client feeling more competent and hopeful about his/her future?
- ◊ Does the client notice how his/her changes are affecting the relationships with other significant people in their lives?

Note that the questions in both models have a similarity even though the emphasis may appear slightly different. Again, the standard for judging the success of therapy is directly connected to whether the therapist and client can respond positively to the questions above: the client does feel better and is acting differently; the problematic behaviors are less frequent, and therefore having less negative impact on others (whether or not the interactional component is explored in therapy). At the juncture where the therapist and client can say "Yes", is the therapy now considered a success? Here the two models diverge again: *For the Brief clinician, the therapy process is now over. For the Experiential clinician, the therapy process may just be beginning!*

In fact, for the Experiential clinician, now that the presenting issue is less potent and overwhelming, the client is freed-up to do deeper inner work. Stopping the therapy process (just because the presenting issue is solved) may be considered by some Experiential practitioners as a mark of shallowness: the client may not have addressed the underlying issues that caused the problem in the first place. If the fundamental issues are not fully addressed, then from an Experiential perspective the changes that the client has made are not likely to last; the issues will simply resurface later on, perhaps in the same context, or more likely in a different guise.

So, how do we know when therapy is finished? And by whose definition - client or therapist? Although it appears that there is a wide gap between the two approaches conceptually, regarding the view of what therapy is and isn't, I believe that there is bridging work to do, and areas in which a more compatible integration can occur. Here are some possible scenarios:

First scenario: A client comes into therapy. His/her funds and/or time are limited. The client wants to solve the problem and move on. In this case, at first glance the Brief Therapy approach would *appear* to be the option of choice - BUT - what if the client has a natural affinity for *process?* What if his/her style of expression is *intuitive, affective,* and *visceral?*

Is this an **integration spot?** Would it be helpful to pose some Solution Oriented questions, but phrased in a more Experiential manner? Might bringing in an Experiential component actually help the therapist and client work better together - and faster?

Second scenario: A client comes into therapy with a less specific and more vague goal: "My mother died two years ago and I can't seem to get over it"; "I have a wonderful family and a good life - yet I'm so unhappy and I just don't know why?" This scenario lends itself perfectly to Experiential work - BUT - what if the client rambles on and on? What if the therapist has trouble helping the client get to the crux of the issue?

Is this an **integration spot?** Would some Experiential suggestions clothed in Solution Oriented questions help the client clarify where s/he would like to be headed in therapy? And maybe develop some short and long-term goals to clarify the direction of the therapy?

Third scenario: A client has completed a round of Brief Therapy. S/he is so satisfied with how helpful the therapy has been that s/he would like to continue; the client would like some coaching to work on other issues. Is the Brief Therapist prepared to work long-term with this client? Can the Brief Therapist view this client as more than a person with another issue to be solved? Is there room in the Brief view to see the client as an individual who wants to continue to grow and change? Is this an **integration spot?**

Final scenario: A client has come to an Experiential therapist. Everything is working: the experiential process suits the client very well; there is a meaningful rapport between the clinician and patient; progress is happening. However, the client's funds are limited; s/he cannot come every week; in fact this client may only be able to come once a month or every five weeks. Is the Experiential therapist prepared to integrate Solution Oriented questions to help the client clarify the process and give the client some specific goals to work on between sessions? Can the Experiential therapist accept that deep change can have a brief orientation? Is this an **integration spot?**

These examples point to areas where I feel further investigation on both sides of the (therapy) coin are needed. The Brief therapist is oriented toward problem resolution – preferably briefly. The Experiential therapist is oriented toward problem exploration – preferably - deeply. I am interested in how to weave and integrate the best from each of these approaches. So I leave the reader to ponder: Is there room in the practice of psychotherapy to draw on *what works,* using the major strengths from each approach?

Who Said That?
Working With Parts

It is best to be with those in time, that we hope to be with in eternity.

Thomas Fuller

Focusing

The relevance of working with *parts* is directly connected to Gendlin's philosophy of wholeness, and fundamental to the practice of Focusing Oriented Psychotherapy.

The theory is as follows: Daily, we go through our routines functioning at multiple levels and utilizing diverse parts of ourselves. There are parts of us that are capable and mature, and other parts that are childish. There are parts that are ingenious and creative, and parts that are too paralyzed to come forth with the simplest idea or coherent thought. There are parts that are focused and productive, and parts that are apathetic and lazy. In this sense we might jokingly say that we are all "multiples"!

What keeps us sane is that most of us have a stable ego-structure that ultimately, even after a very bad day, brings us back to our core-self, center, consciousness, observer (there are many and varied terms).

In Focusing, the various parts are "allowed" or "permitted" to speak and to *be there* – in fact they are warmly welcomed. The work is to help the client *integrate* these various parts into a relatively happy, healthy, functioning whole. If I may share an image, my conception of the co-working of parts looks something like this:

> There is a community of people, all kinds of people: Healthy people, sick people, smart people, not-so-smart people. They are all on a journey together, going to the same place. The ground-rules are that the journey can take as long as it takes with no time limitation; detours are allowable, and in the end if the group cooperates, they will all get where they are going.
>
> The only glitch is that *no one is allowed to be left behind* - either they all go, or nobody goes! If one of the members of the community gets sick (the *part*) everyone has to stop and help him or her heal. When healing occurs (the *part* is well) they can all continue to march on to their destination.

If the Focusing Oriented therapist is working with parts the following components are woven into the session:

- ◊ The therapist *listens*, and teaches clients *how to listen* to the various parts.
- ◊ The client learns how, in a safe and non-judgmental way, to "allow and permit" each of the parts to speak (i.e. be allowed to have their 'say').
- ◊ The therapist facilitates dialogues in which the parts speak to each other.
- ◊ Together, the therapist and client explore ways to find out how the parts can be more supportive of each other.

Solution

In Solution (and most Brief Therapy approaches) there is no explicit discussion of parts, especially in relationship to the Self, e.g., "There's a part of me that wants to, and another part that doesn't..." and yet the whole issue of parts is seamlessly woven into sessions without specifically highlighting them.

The process of working with parts is beautifully and creatively demonstrated by Michael White (1988), the developer of Narrative Therapy (a Brief Therapy approach). His term for the process of working with parts is called "externalizing", i.e., making the part an external condition, separate from the person. Notice in the brief dialogue below, White's Narrative approach with a boy who is getting himself into a lot of trouble at school:

THERAPIST: It looks like *trouble* is giving you some problems...

BOY: Yeah, I might get thrown out of school...

THERAPIST: Would you like to talk about how we can get trouble to back off a bit, so you can see what *you'd* like to do?

What White has done here is almost identical to a Focusing Oriented approach. He labels "trouble" as the problem, and NOT the boy, thereby keeping the boy's Self or 'being' intact (the boy is OK; the "trouble" isn't). Focusing would probably call *trouble* a "part" or "it" ("There's a *part there* that gives you some trouble."). This re-labeling (which separates dysfunction from the core-self) has significant meaning for Experiential therapists, and is congruent with Gendlin's approach and philosophy: There is a core part - Self - that is already "all OK" (the boy)...but then *trouble* gives him some problems.

Note: This is really no different than (at an external level) the example of a child making some trouble for a parent. In theory, if the parent is a wise-adult (synonymous experientially with "Self"), then creative and viable solutions can be explored with the child to help him/her move toward productive change.

The point is that no part can be left behind, killed off, ignored, abused, or abandoned:

◊ In the Experiential framework, genuine healing happens when the disparate parts start becoming integrated into a (relatively) functioning whole. In the Focusing approach, a clear distinction is made between the *I* or *Self* ("Where am *I* in all of this…?") and the *part* (that feels some *other* or resistant way). The issue is *internalized* (hence, the term, "inner parts").

◊ In the Narrative model and other Brief Therapy approaches, finding the "right relationship" is achieved by *externalizing* the part or the issue (such as "trouble"). The result is that the core-self remains separate (and functionally whole) from the problem, or issue.

Whether you are working with parts by internalizing them or externalizing them, it is often helpful to the client to find names that exactly describe (in a *felt* way) who that part is, and what role it plays in the client's life. Some clients describe a child-part as: "the younger one", "the kid", or "the little one". One client I had described the child as "the fragile girl". I have heard: "the sad one", "the angry one", "Mr. Fix-it", "the over-achiever" and "Harry the Horrible". Whatever names the client may give to uniquely describe their inner parts, you will find it very useful, especially when things are going well, and then suddenly get sabotaged by an old scared voice (or critical voice) to be able say to the client: "*Who* said that!" Generally, the three primary "voices" (parts) that emerge most often in a Focusing Oriented context are:

1. The "Self": Sometimes referred to as the "adult", "the authentic voice", "the wise one", "my center place", the "core place"…

2. The "Child" part: A part that got "left behind", with unresolved issues that have been carried into adulthood, so that in certain circumstances the grown adult is "acting out" like a child.

3. The Critic: A part that blames, accuses, and sabotages a person's positive energy, in negative and destructive ways.

This latter one seems to be such a fundamental obstacle for so many people that it is worth a more detailed explanation.

The Critic

The critical faculty has its value in correcting errors, reforming abuses, and demolishing superstitions...but the constructive faculty is...immeasurably more valuable in its results...It is a much nobler and better thing to build up than to pull down.

J.M. Gibson

The Critic exists, to a greater or lesser degree, in every human being. Gendlin views the Critic, or super-ego, as *a part* that has been internalized from early childhood. It is generally a composite of voices, often of primary caretakers and significant early influences: parents, grandparents, teachers, religious influences, and anyone else who may have had a profound effect in a youngster's formative years. The child eventually internalizes the messages as *truth*, whether they were intentionally meant to be negative or not. This is an important point: *the internalization of critical voices has more to do with how a person has taken them in, rather than what actually happened.*

Note: Yes, of course there are cases of serious abuse, or at least parents with un-channeled tempers. Yet even in those circumstances (especially where there is more than one sibling), it is possible that one child has been devastated, while another (or others) emerge into adulthood even stronger – or with a keen desire to be more loving and gentle.

What I am referring to here are instances of relatively 'normal' parents who happen to be having an 'off' day, and utter some thoughtless phrase in exasperation, having no clue whatsoever that the child will internalize the message in a hurtful way. For example, a parent may remark: "If you don't clean up your room, you'll never amount to anything!" All the child takes in is: *"I'll never amount to anything... I'll never amount to anything...I'll never amount to anything..."* Sometimes the stressed-out parent will make an allusion to another sibling: "If you'd be a good boy like your brother..." and the child hears, *"He's good, I'm bad...He's good, I'm bad...He's good, I'm bad..."*

Over time and with growth, this developing inner Critic takes on or assumes many and varied forms, from an authoritarian parent: *Can't you do anything right?* to a testy doubter: *Do you really think you're capable?* The critical voices range from bitter tirades: *You're good for nothing!* to crushing generalities: *How can you always be so stupid?* to sly over concern: *Better be careful...you'll blow it...again.*

I always tell my clients that "the Critic is as smart as you are" (most people think they are smart!) – meaning that the Critic has a myriad of ways and clever tricks to move in on a perfectly wonderful space.

Sometimes the Critic wedges its way in, in moments of doubt, confusion, or uncertainty, especially when a newly-forming idea, project, or relationship is just emerging…the feelings about it are still uncertain and an inner vulnerability exists about whether the idea, project, or relationship is worthwhile. In those fragile moments the Critic can infiltrate our inner space, take some vulnerable part of ourselves and exaggerate or distort it until we are convinced that it must be true. The outcome can feel debilitating: *"You'll never be able to pull this off"* or *"Wait 'til they find out what you're really like…"*

Sometimes a Critic will appear when we are having a perfectly wonderful time to remind us that either: *"This won't last…so don't get your hopes up"* or *"You really don't deserve this."* Sometimes, under the guise of 'protection' the Critic insists that it is intervening for our own good: *"If you bow out now, in the early stages, you won't make a total fool of yourself later."* The results can be paralyzing: we are no longer able to act, or worse, we take very destructive action.

There are innumerable ways to deal with the Critic. If you speak with ten different clinicians you'll hear ten different ways to manage this sometimes unruly part – and probably all of them are right. The bottom line is a) to find a method(s) that feels resonant and effective for the client, and b) to discover what has worked (first hand) for the therapist in dealing with his/her own critical voices. Clearly, what I am presenting here is what has been effective for me personally and in my practice – the rest is trial and error!

Two important factors in managing the Critic are:

- ◊ Learning how to distinguish between what it *is* and what it *isn't*.
- ◊ Paying attention to the *felt-sense of the Self* vs. the *felt-sense of the Critic*. When the Critic speaks, *it always feels terrible.*

When the Self speaks, *it always feels like relief…*

If the feeling inside is *true* and *right*, it is the Self speaking.
Felt-sense: Relief, fresh air, expansive, an inner "Yes!"

When the Critic speaks, it *always feels awful*...

If the feeling inside is *true* but *awful*, it is the Critic speaking.
Felt-sense: Contraction, panic, tight, "up against the wall."

It is important to become familiar with the subtle transitions and tone of the Critic. Sometimes a realization of truth produces a mixed feeling: *The awful truth*:

◊ Something for which we *know* we will have to take responsibility

◊ Something we wish we didn't have to know, or could avoid, yet the feeling inside is still of *relief* and *rightness*.

This is the *voice of wisdom and insight*. The client is asked to "welcome it!"

Some Helpful strategies to teach clients:

◊ Avoid getting "hooked" into dialoguing and arguing with the Critic.

◊ *Stop. Breathe. Get quiet.* Help the client create a safe space for the part that is being beaten up by the Critic; attend to the part immediately.

◊ Try to help the client access the Self in a gentle, non-reactive way, attempting to determine: *What is this really about?*

A usual ploy of the Critic is to keep a person focused on *what is wrong* instead of what *would be right*. For example, if the Critic says, *How could you be so stupid?* or *You really blew it this time!*, help the client separate the *feelings* from the actual *issue:*

◊ *Do I really think that I am stupid?* NO

◊ *Are there some issues that I don't handle well, sometimes?* YES

◊ *Do I think that I didn't handle this issue very well?* YES

◊ *Would I be willing to look at what happened? See if I can learn something from it? Maybe do it in a better way next time?* YES!!

What you have just done is to help the client separate the actual truth from *emotional reactivity*. From the Critic's point of view, the original issue *appeared* to be about the client's mental capabilities: *You're stupid...you blew it.* The actual issue is that the client is disappointed with the way s/he handled an issue. The process of healing involves assisting the client in revisiting the issue freshly in a constructive way, and most importantly, helping the client to see the issue from a *right distance.* This is called "separating the people from the problem" (Fisher and Ury, 1981).

Note: Helping clients access their "adult-self" in order to manage the Critic is essential in diminishing the Critic's intensity and protecting the part that is being attacked. It is very effective to ask clients to imagine that they are dealing with a child who feels remorseful about something s/he has done. The therapist asks the client how, if they loved that child very much, they might respond in that (negative) situation. Typical responses are:

- ◊ Having an attitude of caring and patience.
- ◊ Putting an arm around the child.
- ◊ Speaking in a comforting tone.
- ◊ Listening to the child's feelings, and point of view.
- ◊ Trying to work toward a better solution next time.

Critic attacks are most prevalent when:

- ◊ A person is feeling open, creative, and in a very positive frame of mind. (The client feels s/he doesn't *deserve* to feel this good.)
- ◊ When a new awareness comes that is still fragile, unformed, and needs time and space to grow. (Critic: *Another one of your dumb ideas!*)
- ◊ When a person is feeling vulnerable, touchy, or out of sorts.

Common Critic Ploys:

- ◊ *You need me.*
- ◊ *Who else would tell you this?*
- ◊ *This is for your own good.*
- ◊ *Don't be such a*___(name calling).
- ◊ *I'm only trying to protect you from making a fool of yourself - again.*

The Focusing Oriented therapist teaches the client how to avoid dialoguing with the Critic:

- ◊ *I will not listen to anyone who speaks to me in this tone of voice!*
- ◊ *I'll consider what you said but NOT NOW!*
- ◊ *Thank you for sharing. Good-bye.*

The only acceptable dialogue is between the Self and its parts - from a safe inner place. The Critic is able to get a person's attention in the first place because its statements usually contain some small grain of truth. The problem is that the "grain" is out of context and exaggerated out of all proportion.

Remember: If it sounds true but feels bad, derogatory or condemning, it is the Critic. If it sounds true and feels right, it is the true voice of the Self.

Some helpful distinctions:

Self	Critic
• Respectful	• Attacking
• Soft, gentle	• Harsh, cruel
• Compassionate	• Lacks compassion
• Holistic: sees wider picture	• Fragmented: always points to worst
• Sense of timing: willingness to wait, “Think it over, take your time”	• Pushy: “Do it now, no time to lose; hurry up
• Sounds like a wise teacher, or caring friend	• Sounds like a critical authority, enemy
• Non-judgmental, accepting, empathic, understanding	• Judgmental, critical, lacking empathy and understanding; makes person feel wrong, bad, guilty
• Speaks from within: feels deep and resonant	• Speaks from without; feels like external overwhelming force
• Feels like inner “home”	• Feels like being abandoned or lost

How to Work With the Critic

Focusing Approach

It is important to point out here that there is no "script" in a therapy session for working with the Critic. Some critics are so subtle that the client isn't even aware of its presence.

For example, when we say something in a conversation that we later regret it is quite normal to feel badly about it, i.e., generally no one feels good about inadvertently hurting someone's feelings.

An **appropriate response** is to say to oneself: *"I feel badly that I might have hurt her feelings. I think I'll send a note or pick up the phone and call."*

A critical **inappropriate response** might be: *"Ugghhh are you ever dumb...do you ever say the right thing at the right time??"*

The point: A Critic attacks or ***addresses the person***. A wise Self ***addresses behavior.***

The clinician can do different things at different times. It is very helpful for clinicians to compile a notebook on working with the Critic, filled with assorted interventions that are effective at various junctures in the therapy process. For example:

◇ Psycho-education

For new clients, it is often helpful to explain a bit about *parts*.

We all have many parts: child-like parts, creative parts, adult parts, and critical parts. I often use the example of a child making a mistake: Imagine that the child has failed his math test, and feels just awful about it. I might then ask the client how likely is it that s/he would say to the child: *"You are the stupidest kid I've ever known, you are going to be a failure in life, and I don't love you anymore..."* then maybe giving the kid a spanking.

The client is of course totally horrified by the example, and I often point out that in real-time this is called "child abuse" and it is illegal. I explain that inner abuse is psychologically and spiritually "illegal" and is not OK - EVER! I then ask the client what they might say if a child that s/he loved very much came in distraught and crying about the failed math test.There are lots of variations, but in most cases the scenario looks something like this:

The child comes in crying; the client holds or hugs the child and acknowledges that the child clearly feels terrible about having done so poorly on the test. The client is then coached to ask the child: *If that child could speak to you, right now, is there anything that s/he would want to say to you?* The answers (from the "child") may include needing support and encouragement, asking for patience and kindness, needing to feel loved and be held, or perhaps getting some extra help in math (if this is a difficult subject).

The point is that the interaction takes place between a supportive adult, and a part that needs the support. There is no place for a Critic in the interaction, except perhaps to acknowledge to the Critic, *Yes, there is a part of me that blew it, thank you for sharing. I'll handle it.*

This kind of powerful example can transform the way a client sees his/her Critic. In subsequent sessions, when a Critic intrudes, the therapist will be able to ask:

- *Is this how you would really talk to a child that you love?*
- *Do you think this tone sounds a bit harsh?*
- *Whose voice is that anyway? It doesn't sound like You!*

◇ Experiential

If you want to try a more process-oriented approach, here are some useful exercises that can be adapted to suit your style.

Exercise One:

Have the client close his/her eyes. Ask him/her to begin to notice the voice of the Critic, how loud or soft the pitch of the voice is, and where it is located. *Critics almost always speak from behind* the person or *off to the side*. Then ask the client to bring the Critic around in front to face him/her, to see what the Critic looks like. This produces some very interesting images:

◊ The Critic appears as veiled or cloaked and is not recognizable.

◊ The Critic appears as some weird or evil creature - something out of Tolkien or Star Trek.

◊ The Critic looks like mom, dad, teacher, sibling, or some actual person from the past.

The therapist and client explore: *Who* is under the costume? It is often a terrified child, hiding out from the feelings of psychological (and in some cases physical) abuse.

Then, the therapist facilitates a dialogue between the client and the Critic.

Note: This dialogue should be coached by the therapist. Unless the client is very skilled in dealing with the Critic, and very aware of the subtle ways it attacks, s/he should not be encouraged to dialogue with the Critic outside of the therapy room.

Ask the client to ask the Critic: *Who are you? What do you want?*

Here the Critic often explains that it is trying to be helpful: *"I'm just trying to protect you from being so stupid and blowing it again."* This is a good place to use *reframing:* the clinician works with the client to explain to the Critic that while *being protected* is appreciated, the manner in which the Critic is doing it is not helpful at all, and *"We'll need to do this in a new way..."*

Exercise Two:

Guide the client back to a time when s/he first sensed the presence of the Critic. *What was that like?* The client will usually describe a most unpleasant and constricted felt-sense. Work with the felt-sense to find out what it needs *now* to feel free of the bad feeling:

◊ *Can you sense what feels like…fresh air?*

◊ *See if there's anything that might feel like relief…here…*

◊ *What do you sense is needed…to make some healing…*

Finally, keep in mind that if we look to physics we know that "energy cannot be created or destroyed" - only transformed. Hence, we cannot kill or destroy the Critic. We can, however, give it another more useful 'job' (than beating us up!)

Ask the client to think about, and sense what a *transformation* of critical energy might look like, i.e. other *useful purposes* that the Critic might serve if it did have a *different job* or was *doing its job differently.*

For example, the 'job' of the Critic is a form of protection (distorted as that may be). The Critic, by nature, is *critical:* it tells us what's wrong. However, it seems to me, that if we *deleted the nastiness*, meaning: separating the message from the messenger, or the intent of the message from the delivery, having a 'critical faculty' might indeed be a very useful life tool - and - we just might come up with some new, valuable, and interesting "characters". I offer here two of mine – reframed!

"The Friendly Devil's Advocate": This one is sort of like a lawyer. Its job is to do exactly what a good lawyer should do: point out the risks, point out the advantages, point out where caution is necessary, discuss various options – AND – let me go home and think about it without pressure!

I don't mind having a lawyer (my actual lawyer is a very nice guy). He advises me, kindly. He doesn't tell me I'm stupid. He simply points out the pros and cons, gives me his best advice, and then allows some time to make my own decisions. I don't mind having a "Friendly Devil's Advocate" in my (inner) cast of characters!

"The Discerner": This is actually one of my favorite characters (*parts*) and we treat each other with the utmost respect. This Discerner is TOTALLY OBJECTIVE. It has no emotional quality at all (*I do*, but '*it' doesn't!*). The Discerner is the keeper of right boundaries. I can *sense* its messages and decide whether or not they *feel right*. This part is a first-rate observer, and carefully identifies and/or labels what *is so* with the most accurate objectivity it is capable of mustering. Example: When I write, the Discerner is "on call". It says things like: *"Good job, that works...delete that...this doesn't fit here...cut and paste this one to a different place."* It doesn't say, *"You've got to be kidding, that's really awful writing, are you ever dumb."*

The point: Energy cannot be created or destroyed, but it can be transformed. Take the time to let the client (or yourself!) internalize another job for the Critic that would be more useful, helpful, constructive, and supportive.

In closing, we teach and practice therapy out of what comes most naturally to us. *The best way to work with clients is from our direct experience*. Experiment with your own critical voices. See what works most effectively for you. Each of us has a *highly individualized Critic!*

Solution Approach

The Solution Oriented therapist also deals with *parts*, usually in the form of facilitating a dialogue in which the *parts* learn how to cooperate more usefully with each other (this will be covered in depth in the section called "Dialoguing").

In addition, the Solution Oriented therapist also pays attention to the negative aspects of the personality, although the term Critic is not specifically used. In lieu of dealing directly with the Critic, the Solution approach uses certain linguistic techniques to avoid critical influences. All Brief Therapy models are precise in their use of language. The way sentences are phrased, intentionally emphasizing some words while de-emphasizing others, is a direct outgrowth of the work of Milton Erickson. Erickson's manner of speaking and phrasing sentences was influenced by his use of hypnosis in therapy.

One of the theories behind hypnosis is that the subconscious mind cannot register negative words such as: "don't", "can't", "not", and "won't". Thus, if a client says, "I don't want to be so sloppy", the only part of that sentence that the subconscious mind will hear is "*be so sloppy"*. Over and over again, unknowingly, the client is programming him/her self to *be so sloppy…be so sloppy.* What will help the client re-program more consciously is to state, in the affirmative, what he or she does want: "I want to be neater."

It is therefore essential for the therapist to point the client toward what *is* wanted, rather than what *isn't* wanted:

Don't want	Want
I don't want to lose my temper	*I want to handle my anger*
I don't want to fail	*I want to succeed*
I don't want to be so fat	*I want to lose weight*
I don't want to procrastinate	*I want to get things done*

If the Critic states the sentence in the affirmative, such as, "I always put my foot in my mouth" or "I'm such a jerk", then the therapist needs to explore with the client, "See what you would *like to have happen instead?"* until the client can find the right words: "I *want* to learn to think before I speak" or "I *want* to choose my words more carefully".

The therapist may also rephrase what the client has said:

> CLIENT: I hate the way my life is going. I hate myself...nothing works…and I blow it all the time with that temper of mine.

> THERAPIST: So you really *want* change. You *want* to work toward a time, *when you are calmer,* when you *are being* and *acting* just the *way you want* to...when *you are liking yourself.*

There are times when a client's Critic is so pervasive, that simply ignoring it minimizes the powerful impact that the Critic has on the client's life and view of him/herself. In situations where the Critic refuses to go away, it may be helpful to coach a dialogue between the client and the Critic.

Note: The format is identical to the usual Solution Oriented approach to negotiating an agreement or compromise between any two people who are not getting along.

What needs to be explored is:

- ◊ What each party (or *part*) wants.
- ◊ What each can do that will be helpful to the other.
- ◊ What difference it will make to the client when the Critic is giving more helpful advice, in a less critical manner.
- ◊ What difference it will make to the Critic when the client is behaving differently.
- ◊ In what areas the client and the Critic can support each other more.
- ◊ Finding one specific thing (until the next session) that the Critic can do that will make a real difference to the client - and vice versa - one specific thing that the client can do that will make a real difference to the Critic.
- ◊ Again, re-naming the Critic with a title that has a more useful function will be very helpful to the client.

One of the key factors in working with the Critic is to understand that no matter how skewed or distorted, the Critic really believes that its role is to protect the client from 'something' - usually some form of inappropriate behavior. When the client begins to genuinely grasp that there are more useful and positive ways to feel protected (than succumbing to the critical voice), the relationship between the client and Critic will change.

Although we are talking here about the internal relationship to the Critic, keep in mind that the same principles apply to working externally with critical others. In both the Solution and Focusing models, sentences are rephrased in a more constructive and palatable way:

You don't communicate with me
becomes
It means so much to me when you share your thoughts with me.

You always do that
becomes
It would help me a lot if you could do __X__ instead.

You're so insensitive
becomes
I'd really appreciate it if you'd take my point of view into consideration.

While both models emphasize a more positive manner of relating, the motivation is slightly different:

Focusing emphasizes congruency between the body and mind. The body says it wants to feel good. The critical mind says, *You can't feel good because you're bad.* The "Focusing Attitude" which is the antithesis of the Critic, is the essential healing factor. Treating the Self and others with respect and dignity is a natural prescription for working with the Critic.

Solution steers clients away from critical voices by concentrating on the *effect of language* in a positive way. Through continual modeling by the therapist, who repeatedly points clients toward what they want, clients learn how to turn away from a negative thought process, and concentrate instead on what they want and what is possible.

Psycho-Education

The aim of education should be to teach us rather how to think, than what to think.

James Beattie

Here is an interesting paradox:

Focusing

Focusing Oriented Therapy is an *internal* process. The therapist is hyper-vigilant about being non-intrusive, and non-directive - yet, practitioners explicitly *teach* anything and everything that will help the client do better in therapy.

Solution

Solution Oriented Therapy is an *external* process. The therapist, although respectful, may be quite straightforward and directive - yet, practitioners *don't teach* anything at all, or rarely. In fact, there are some clinicians who consider psycho-education intrusive and disrespectful.

INTEGRATION SPOT

Teaching is an area where Focusing can add something very worthwhile to the Solution approach. Clients often find considerable value in learning more about aspects of their therapy experience, especially when what they learn is directly relevant to better understanding their own behavioral patterns, and helpful solutions that will lead them toward change.

Teaching creates a common language between the therapist and the client, and fits perfectly with Gendlin's idea of showing clients how to be better clients. Whether I am using Focusing, Solution, or a combination of both, I often stop to explain what I am saying and why. Most of my clients know all or some of the following:

◊ How to listen, internally and externally, and the skills involved in successful interactions including the difference between: *I-statements* and *you-statements.*

◊ What the *felt-sense* is; respecting inner wisdom and bodily knowing.

◊ How to be in *right relationship* with an issue.

◊ About the parts (Self, Child, Critic) and learning to identify which one of them is speaking: *Who said that?*

◊ Inner safety: how to get and keep it; understanding the difference between *unsafe* (which is intolerable) and *uncomfortable* (which is manageable).

◊ How to maintain a respectful *attitude* toward the Self and others, especially when the Critic intrudes.

◊ How to use language in a positive way: what I do want, rather than what I don't want.

The process of teaching, (as distinct from modeling) is not for everyone, and may feel foreign to some Brief Therapists. However, the value can be immeasurable for clients; and it takes little effort on the part of the therapist.

Teaching weaves the knowledge of the client and the therapist together in a process which happens gently and naturally over time. Naming and labeling helps clients remember. Spontaneous insight is a powerful and moving experience. Sometimes, when the client is beating him/her self up, he/she will suddenly look up and say, "Wow! I'm having a Critic attack, aren't I?" or "Now I know what you mean about needing to protect that *part!"*

What has happened is that the client has now internalized the information. The client has independently named the problem, or at least part of it. Clients are generally thrilled with their insights (and so am I!).

INTEGRATION: Develop a common language with clients. Help them name and label what is going on in their internal process, as well as in their interactions with others. *Clients appreciate education, especially when the subject is them!*

How the Approaches are Different and Complementary

I am not struck so much by the diversity of testimony as by the many-sidedness of truth.

Stanley Baldwin

Change

Solution

All Brief Therapy is centered around the concept of change, and uses a variety of interventions and techniques to help clients move the change process toward solutions. The Brief Therapy approaches remain anchored in the positive while seeking to resolve the presenting problem.

The Solution Oriented practitioner is interested in effecting change in the areas identified by the client, and explores with the client the solutions that may - or may not - be related to the presenting problem(s). This is an important point: The *solution* is what is emphasized rather than the problem. The therapist and client work together to co-create new behaviors and action steps that will support the client in the process of change.

Note: In both Focusing and Solution these action steps are referred to as "small, manageable steps"; they are built upon progressively according to the client's sense of *what works* or *what feels right*. The therapist can also help facilitate change by observing what the client is *already doing* that works, pointing out these practices, and building upon them with supportive and congruent action steps.

Focusing

All Experiential models seek to help clients experience what they are feeling in the here-and-now. A significant difference between the Experiential and Brief Therapy approaches is in their emphasis. The Experiential approach is more focused on personal growth and inner change, than on symptom relief. While relief from the presenting issue is considered important, it holds a second place to what we might loosely call *being true to oneself* or having inner integrity. More specifically, the therapist helps clients learn how to experience congruency between what they are feeling and what they are thinking. In Focusing Oriented therapy, the two must *match.* I sometimes refer to congruency as "think/feel".

Of course, Experiential work promotes and produces change, but change needs to be accompanied by *experiential understanding*: the bodily felt "Aha! Phenomenon" (Littlewood, 1992) or "Gestalt" (Perls, 1969).

In his 1959 article "A Tentative Scale for the Measurement of Process in Psychotherapy", Carl Rogers states very beautifully his own strongly-held feelings about the value of "experiencing":

> *...It involves being in an unknown flow rather than in a clear structure...there is, in the act of experiencing, a referent which can be symbolized and checked or rechecked for its further meanings and symbolizations. There is a strong desire for exactness in these conceptualizations. There may be a dim realization that living in terms of these solid referents would be possible...There is full acceptance now of experiencing as providing a clear and usable referent for getting at the implicit meanings of the individual's encounter with himself and with life...the recognition that the self is now becoming this process of experiencing.*

The following case demonstrates how the Focusing Oriented therapist helps the client better understand her inner experience. Notice, as the session progresses, how the client shifts from a raw emotion to a holistic, bodily felt-sense.

SUSAN: Ughhh, I'm just *so angry* about the fight I had with John.

THERAPIST: There's a lot of anger *there*...Would it be alright to take a minute to back up...just a little...so you can *sense yourself* as a bit *separate* from all that anger...maybe just breathe a little...

It is not possible to be *in* an emotion and *have* an emotion at the same time; one cannot have a felt-sense *of* the problem if one is *in* the problem. If the client can't separate from the intense feelings, if there is no Self present to help manage, support, and console the angry-part, then it's as though there is "nobody home" to deal with the problem. In this case, *anger* is the prevailing emotion. Emotions are much more difficult to cope with than felt-senses because they are sharp, harsh, and sometimes feel unbearable.

The therapist's use of the word "there" (which is an abbreviated term for there *in the body*) is a subtle pointer towards the budding formation of a felt-sense.

The suggestion to "back up a little" and "separate" from the anger moves Susan toward the I/it relationship. The therapist is trying to help her find her competent, whole Self, the "I", by creating a separation from "it" (the anger).

SUSAN: (takes a minute to breath and back up a bit) OK...I think I'm here now.

THERAPIST: So...can you just say gently to yourself a couple of times, *All about the fight I had with John... that big whole thing about the fight with John, and all that was in it...*and just see what wants to come in your body.

(Gendlin says it takes at least 30 seconds for the felt-sense to form.)

SUSAN: (after sitting with it for a bit): This isn't the first time, you know... I've had this same fight...about this same thing with John before.

THERAPIST: So this is really familiar to you...you've experienced these same feelings before...around all this stuff with John.

SUSAN: Yes...and it always leaves me feeling this exact same way...(takes a moment to sense it)...like this paralysis in my stomach...a really hard knot...

The felt-sense is beginning to take shape. Remember, the felt-sense is the body's way of registering the *whole picture*: the memories, the images and feelings of the memories, her tight stomach in those memories, all the fights with John over the years about this same issue, and all the anger it produced in her.

THERAPIST: Always the same feeling *there*...like a paralysis…a really hard knot in your stomach…

SUSAN: (nods affirmatively): John is so verbally clever…I can't even begin to think the way he thinks...he has a way of twisting around my words....

THERAPIST: There's some way that he's so clever…something you can't relate to...a way that your words get twisted around…that leaves you…

SUSAN: (gropes for a minute): Like…losing…I always get left with this feeling like I lose…like he wins and I lose…

Her words are now coming directly from the felt-sense, and she is very close to the crux of the matter.

THERAPIST: It's like this win/lose thing…and you always get left feeling like you lose…and that does something to you inside…

SUSAN: Yes…a cringing feeling…You know what I'm seeing now? (pauses as she develops the image) I see a boot…it's a big boot…like a big army boot... and I see a tiny little bug on the ground…and this boot…you know…it just squashes that bug flat out into the ground. Oh my God, that's it!...When I'm with John I feel like a squashed bug!

This spontaneous *knowing* is called a "felt-shift' or the "Aha!" experience - that moment where truth simply is.

Notice the progression from the harsh emotion "I'm so angry" to the felt-sense of "a squashed bug", which is her *visual* and *felt representation* of the whole issue. The imagery here is so rich; it contains everything that Susan needs to move towards "fresh air". As she continues working with the felt-sense of the squashed bug, she will discover that she has several choices:

- ◊ She may leave the relationship.
- ◊ She may get a pair of "boots" of her own, and kick back.
- ◊ She may do something new, to get them on a "more even footing" (no pun intended!)

By *staying with* ("keeping company") and paying attention to the felt-sense of her experience, Susan will discover exactly what is needed to feel less squashed and more like herself. By listening to the felt-sense she will learn how to take the next right steps.

Listening / Questioning

There are ways of doing more than listening, but they aren't 'more' if you do them without listening!

Eugene T. Gendlin

Focusing

In addition to tracking the felt-sense, Susan's case also illustrates the Focusing Oriented approach to listening. The therapist in this approach is not merely listening to and reflecting back the client's words. The therapist attempts, through an empathic and caring connection, to sense the *felt-meaning* behind Susan's words. By being willing to move with a client in whatever direction s/he may want to explore, the therapist is energetically available to do what Gendlin refers to as "experiential listening": *the therapist is listening from his or her own felt-sense.* The manner in which the therapist responds to the client is called the "experiential response" (Gendlin, 1968).

Solution

The Solution Oriented therapist is also a skilled listener; in fact, the word "masterful" is equally accurate. However, the style of listening is quite different, and so is its purpose. Rather than listening *to,* the therapist is listening *for* - the specific junctures where something new is possible:

◊ a change in thinking and viewing that will give the client a different perception of the problem

◊ a place to insert a question that will put the client on a different and more positive track

◊ a place to include others who might be helpful to the client

In other words, listening comes out of questioning. *The type of question asked in the Solution model is as crucial to the successful outcome of therapy, as the listening response is in the Focusing model.*

Consider a replay of Susan's dialogue with her therapist, this time with a Solution Orientation:

(Case: Susan...revisited)

SUSAN: Ughhh, I'm just *so angry* about the fight I had with John.

THERAPIST: You are really going through a rough time in your relationship, right now.

Choosing these words "going through a rough time", instead of reflecting back the anger, helps to defuse the strong emotional component.

SUSAN: I sure am - this guy is driving me crazy!

THERAPIST: You sound very fed up.

For the moment, the therapist shifts the attention from John being the problem, to Susan's ownership of the problem.

SUSAN: Damn right - I've just had enough!

THERAPIST: I'm wondering...when was the last time it was right with John?

The therapist totally shifts gears here; she wants to know a bit more about the relational component.

SUSAN: Hmmm…let me see...we've been together for three years now, and I'd say that the first two years were pretty good…terrific really…before it started going downhill.

THERAPIST: What was different *then*, in the first two years…from how it is *now?*

The therapist is looking for the *exception* to the problem.

SUSAN: Well, for one thing he was traveling, you know, for business…a lot more than he is now.

THERAPIST: Hmmmm…

SUSAN: And because he was away so much...well…we just couldn't get enough of each other when he came home.

THERAPIST: So it was that you got to miss each other. When he would come back you were together in a very intense way, then he would leave again, and you had a complete break from being in relationship.

SUSAN: Exactly! In fact it was like a honeymoon, over and over again…so much passion…and then he'd go off on another trip.

THERAPIST: It sounds as if something has changed.

The therapist is weeding out *what works* from what doesn't work.

SUSAN: It certainly has…He was transferred back home last year, and now he's around all the time.

THERAPIST: I see…so the way you spend your time together is very different now.

The therapist is making a distinction between when it was "good" and how the relationship is "different" now. The word "now" implies a possibility for change in the future.

SUSAN: I never get to miss him any more. He's around just about every night, so I feel that I should be around too…

THERAPIST: I'm wondering…when John was traveling more…what did you do with your time?

The therapist is looking for what *she* was doing differently.

SUSAN: Oh, lots of things. I went to the gym about four times a week, which I hardly ever do any more…and I visited with girlfriends, went to movies…let me see…I took three different courses in a two year period...I read a lot more…

THERAPIST: I'm wondering…if John was here with us now, what do you imagine he'd say about all of this…?

SUSAN: Umm…I think he'd say that it was more romantic before…that it's really changed this past year…

THERAPIST: So he would say something has changed in the romance department… What else do you imagine he'd say...?

SUSAN: I think he'd say that I've changed in some way…(thoughtful)

THERAPIST: You're saying that John would say that *you've* changed in some way…

SUSAN: I guess I have…wow…I was thinking that John had changed so much… especially because he's gotten so much more grumpy and irritable…but now I'm wondering…how I've changed…

THERAPIST: How do you imagine…John would say you've changed?

SUSAN: Ummm…I think he'd say that he thought I was more fun…more interesting before…he'd say I always had so much to say…so many interesting stories to tell…Oh, wow!…what am I saying?…Oh my!…I'm saying that *he'd say* I'm different in the relationship now!

THERAPIST: And what's your own sense about that…?

SUSAN: (pauses to consider the question) I think there's truth to it. I think I've made some assumptions about what John expects of me…but I've never actually asked him…

THERAPIST: OK…let's ask him, now…if John was here with us…and we asked him, *John, what do you think is something Susan could do that would make a difference to you in the way your relationship is going?*…what do you think he'd say?

SUSAN: I think he'd say that he wants us to renegotiate our time together. I think he'd say that he loves being with me…he thinks I'm fun, and funny…but that he also wants me to have a life of my own…to continue to take courses…to do stuff for myself…

THERAPIST: So he'd say he wants you to continue to do things for yourself... (she nods affirmatively)...and is there anything you would want him to do differently...anything that would make the relationship better for you?

SUSAN: I think I need to ask him to communicate more about his needs. It's a big adjustment for him being home...an adjustment for both for us...his new position at work is also an adjustment... I really think he's going through quite a lot, right now...

THERAPIST: It sounds as if John has changed too...

SUSAN: I think he's trying to work out how we should be together...but he's not always good about communicating his needs...Sometimes he just gets very snippy with his words...and it makes me so angry...

THERAPIST: So you want him to communicate with you in a better way...and how do you imagine that will make a difference for you...?

Notice how the therapist has just bypassed the anger.

SUSAN: I think I'd stop making assumptions about what's going on with him... like that he *needs* me to be there for him all the time...I need to ask him more clearly...and I need him to be clearer with me...I need to tell him that...that I want him to be clearer with me.

THERAPIST: So what you're saying is...that when you are doing some of the things you used to do when he was away...and when he's communicating better with you...that is...when you've discussed together how you both want your relationship to be...something will change...

SUSAN: Yes, it will...we really get along quite well together...but we also need breaks...to have things to tell each other...It's so clear now...I'm amazed I didn't see it before!

Comments:

The relationship between Susan and John got back on track. They had never actually discussed how the relationship would look living together on a full time basis. Susan had made assumptions about what John wanted, but they had not actually communicated about it. They negotiated a clearer pattern between doing things separately and doing things together. Susan began to ask John more directly about what he was wanting and needing, and John became more open about communicating his needs. The therapist worked with Susan on the interactional components of the relationship rather than her feelings of anger (as in the Focusing model).

There are two important points to make regarding the orientation that each model takes toward Susan's case:

Focusing

First, the Focusing model approaches the case in terms of Susan's feelings, and her own relationship to herself; the relationship with John is secondary. It is significant that the subject of John never emerged in the interview, except as it related to Susan's feelings about John. In this model an assumption is made by the therapist: by coming to terms with her own feelings, and being clear about where she is, (in Focusing terms, "Where are *you* in all of this?") she will *experientially know* what to do next in relation to John. The next steps will be right steps because she is operating from her own truthful felt-sense of the situation with John.

Solution

When we revisit the case from a Solution perspective, we notice first and foremost, that the approach is based on an important systemic principle: The *interpersonal* orientation (as opposed to the *intrapersonal* orientation of Focusing) inherently assumes that we are always in relationship to someone else; we do not live in a vacuum. Therefore, the therapist wants to know, *How does John fit in here?*

Although we each have our own feelings regarding an issue, the interaction between people in a relationship (whether two individuals or an entire family or group) is essential to understanding the impact on the system as a whole. Hence, the session takes into account the relationship to John, whether or not he is in the room - a very common practice for systemic therapists.

Focusing

Second, in the Focusing Oriented approach (and most Experiential models), *change happens in the therapy room.* The therapist is often witness to profound personal changes, felt-shifts, and "Aha's!" that happen through the process of *processing,* so to speak.

The **value** of experiencing a shift in awareness during the course of a session lies in the deep and shared connection between the therapist and client. The bond, or relationship that forms during therapy plays an integral part in the healing process. The client feels affirmed, valued, and ultimately independent.

Solution

In the Solution Oriented approach (and most Brief models) the therapist is concerned about the *change that happens outside the therapy room.* Of course, clients experience insight, change, and shifts in awareness. However, the therapist is less preoccupied about change happening during the session, unless it happens naturally (as it actually did in Susan's case). The therapist is more interested in what kind of changes will occur outside the therapy room in the interlude between sessions.

The **value** in clients making change outside of the session is that they feel more competent and independent. While a good working relationship develops during the course of therapy, the clinician does everything possible to empower clients, so that they feel capable of handling daily life well - on their own.

My preference here is not either/or, but both/and.

Language

Language is the dress of thought.

Samuel Johnson

Both the Focusing and Solution Oriented models have their own unique way of phrasing or *clothing* questions for a desired effect. At a cursory glance it may seem as if these questions would surely steer clients in entirely different directions. What is astounding is that the final outcome is the same!

Focusing

Focusing Oriented language is expressed in the present tense. It is focused on what the client is experiencing *in the moment:*

- ◊ Can you take a moment *now* to sense what's there for you...
- ◊ Of those three issues, can you sense which has the most energy for you, *right now...*
- ◊ Ask yourself: What *is it* that gives me this uncomfortable feeling…?

The **value** of phrasing questions in the present is that the client can experience the issue freshly and with aliveness, as the body carries it *now* - rather than having the client recount the problem as s/he remembers it from yesterday.

Further, in keeping with the philosophy of Focusing it is only *in-the-moment* that we are able to change and transform our relationship to "it" (the problem, issue, or felt-sense).

Solution

Solution Oriented language is expressed in the future tense. It is directed toward new possibilities:

- ◊ When it is right, what *will* it look like?
- ◊ What *will* be different for you when this is happening?
- ◊ How *will* you be different when this is happening?

The orientation of these questions is always toward creating and building the *Solution Picture.*

Certain key words are used frequently and with emphasis: *will, what, when, yet,* and *then.*

- ◊ How *will* it be for you *when* you are feeling less depressed and more positive?
- ◊ Although it hasn't happened *yet*, imagine a time in the future *when* the problem is solved.
- ◊ *What will* you be doing, *then?*

The **value** in this approach is that it assumes change; the expectation of change is already inherent in the question. The future tense points the client in the direction of unexplored possibilities: "How it *will* be *when* these new changes occur?"

Both models use language with specific intention:

Focusing language is intentionally vague, fuzzy and unclear:

- ◊ "Something about that issue *leaves you feeling...*"
- ◊ "You're saying…it's *something like*…sad…"

If the client says, "Well, it's not exactly sad…" the therapist says,

- ◊ "So it's *not exactly* sad…*it's more like...*"

The therapist intentionally leaves lots of blanks and pauses for uncertainty in order to help the client find the felt-sense: "So it's *something like...*"

The **value** of using vague and fuzzy language lies in the wide scope it gives to the client. Clients receive a strong message of empowerment:

- ◊ The client has space to internally *grope* for the exact right word that fits their *felt-meaning*.
- ◊ The client is invited to spend time with an issue, giving more depth and meaning to his/her experience.
- ◊ The client is able to directly experience congruency between thinking and feeling.

Solution language is *intentionally* specific and precise:

- ◊ "*What exactly will be* the first signs that *will let you know* that this is no longer a problem?"
- ◊ "*What will be happening then,* that isn't happening now?"
- ◊ "*Then what?*"
- ◊ "*What else?*"

The therapist concentrates on developing future possibilities:

"What *will* be happening *when*...?"

The **value** of using specific and precise language lies in helping clients zoom in with more clarity, on both the issue and the solution. Clients receive a strong message of empowerment:

- ◊ Clients become more aware of their goals and expectations.
- ◊ Out of the client's responses will come the specific "action steps" that will help move them toward their goals.
- ◊ Clients learn to discern between what they can and can't do.

What is extraordinary about these different approaches to language is that both are designed to take the client to the *exact same place* in terms of producing change.

Focusing: By using vague and fuzzy language, the Focusing Oriented therapist helps the client *pin down exactly what stands in the way* between the client and the action step.

Solution: By using clear and precise language, the Solution Oriented therapist helps the client *pin down exactly* what the action step *will be* between now and the next session.

Solution: goes directly to the action step while Focusing takes into account any obstacles to reaching the action step, but *they both get to the action step!*

Who Else is in the Picture?

It is good to rub and polish our brain against that of others.
Montaigne

Solution

The Solution Oriented model considers clients in the context of his/her relationships. Problems and issues are observed in terms of patterns of interaction, circularity in the system, and how each person has an impact upon the other(s) in the relationship. Because the inclusion of others is so fundamental to this model, the presence of others is built directly into the language, even if the therapist is only working with one client:

- ◊ "So who will be the first to notice the changes you are making?...Who else?"
- ◊ "What will let you know that your wife has noticed these changes?"
- ◊ "What will she be telling you, then, that she is not telling you now?"

Referring again to Susan, note how the Solution Oriented therapist brought John into the picture:

- ◊ When were things good with him?
- ◊ What needed to change for their relationship to be good again?
- ◊ What could she do differently in relation to him?

Wherever possible, the Solution Oriented approach takes into account the presence of significant others - the relationships.

Focusing

Experiential work has traditionally been based on psychodynamic models which are rooted in personal unfoldment, individual development and self-exploration, or as Rogers would say, "self-actualization." Therefore, the Focusing Oriented approach is less concerned with the inclusion of others, and pays more attention to the client's inner relationship: the *Self* in relation to its various *parts*.

- ◊ "Ask inside, *How does that feel to me, right now?*"
- ◊ "If the felt-sense could speak...is there anything it wants you to know?"
- ◊ "One part of you really wants to go...but another part feels some resistance around that."

In the Focusing model wellness and healing are dependent upon the integration of parts into the whole: Each part has a working relationship with the core Self; inner balance is maintained and sustained through healthy inner dialogue and the process of listening within.

INTEGRATION SPOT

We come again to a place where integration, inclusion, and a both/and perspective are needed.

Implicit in the Focusing model is the question:

◊ *Who am I in relationship to myself?*

Implicit in the Solution model is the question:

◊ *Who am I in relationship to you?*

Frankly, I do not believe that the two questions can be separated, or said another way, each is right at the appropriate moment.

On one hand, we don't live in a vacuum. Most of the issues that clients present have to do with feelings, reactions, and responses in relation to someone else. Therefore the question, *Who am I in relationship to you?* is generally an operative one.

On the other hand, who I perceive myself to be in relationship to you is probably directly connected with, *Who I am in relationship to myself?* If the inner relationship is healthy, I know who I am and therefore I know how to be in relationship to you. Further, I can recognize myself as a *separate* entity from who you are: I can be my most genuine *me* in relationship to *you*.

However, if some part of the inner relationship is dysfunctional, disconnected, or ruled by a false-self, for example top-heavy with critical influences, the client may *project* qualities or motives on to another person that don't actually exist in the other person, e.g., being overly defensive in response to feed-back (versus criticism), but which the client perceives as criticism.

Hence, when we are exploring with our clients *Who else is in the picture?* we need to pose the question at several levels: *Who is me? Who is you? Who are we?*

Dialoguing

He (or she) who knows only his (or her) own side of the case knows little of that.

(Adapted from John Stuart Mill)

A dialogue is a conversation. A conversation implies communication, which in turn implies relationship. In order to understand how relationships work, it is helpful to examine *how* people communicate. Both the Solution and Focusing Oriented models regard the intricacies and dynamics of interaction as essential to a good working relationship, whether or not the dialogue is focused internally or externally.

Conversations can take a number of forms: dialoguing with one's Self, dialoguing between couples or within families, dialoguing with people who are not actually in the room, and of course, dialoguing with the therapist during the course of a session.

Focusing

The Focusing Oriented model, with its emphasis on being present to, and in touch with the Self, tends to *internalize* the dialogue, so that the conversation takes place between the Self and its parts. Further, the Focusing Oriented therapist will often avoid the use of direct questions with clients in order to encourage them to *ask themselves.*

For example, let's imagine that the question that the therapist would really like to ask is, "What do you plan to do about it?" In Focusing Oriented language the question might be phrased like this:

> "Can you ask yourself: *So what's my sense of what needs to happen, right now...a right next step that would fit for me?"*

Or the therapist may want to ask, "What is the cause of all this pain?" This might be verbalized as follows:

> "Can you ask this inside place to sense... *What is this pain connected to in my life, right now?* Or, *What is it that makes all this discomfort in here?"*

The following case illustrates the Focusing Oriented approach to inner dialogue.

Victor is 18 years old. He is shy, insecure, and has a difficult time communicating with people. His Critic is strong, and his sense of Self is fragile.

VICTOR: I'm such a terrible communicator.

THERAPIST: It sounds as if there's a part of you that has trouble communicating.

VICTOR: Sometimes I'm so tongue tied...I feel like an idiot.

The I/it relationship has not yet been established. At the moment, Victor doesn't *have* the problem; he *is* the problem.

THERAPIST: It sounds like there are two parts of you…one part that really wants to communicate better, and another part that has a lot of trouble with that…

He quietly considers what the therapist has said.

THERAPIST: Would it be alright...to just take a minute to sense both parts…the part that wants to and the part that doesn't?

VICTOR: (after a moment): Oh, I just hate that part.

His Critic has just intruded on the process.

THERAPIST: Sounds like a Critic in there…let's imagine that there was no Critic… just a part that was feeling kind of awful at the moment…something like a scared child that you cared about a lot…See if there is anything you sense might be right to do here…

VICTOR: If I really had a child that felt like I feel…well…I'd probably give him a hug…and try to comfort him…

THERAPIST: So that part needs comforting…Can you take just a moment with yourself to do that…

VICTOR: That feels good…it feels right…

THERAPIST: So this part needs comfort…and really wants to communicate better, but he doesn't know how...

VICTOR: He gets tongue tied and scared…

THERAPIST: Sometimes he gets tongue-tied and scared…maybe…he needs your help in some way…Could you could ask yourself, *If that scared part could speak to me, right now, is there anything he would like me to know?*

The therapist encourages him to ask himself.

VICTOR: That part says…he wants me to be nicer to him...he says I make him feel terrible.

THERAPIST: So that part…he…wants you to be nicer to him…

VICTOR: When I was a child, I used to stutter. I don't stutter any more…but there's an old fear…like my words might get jumbled like they used to…that I'll say something stupid, and make a fool of myself.

THERAPIST: So there is an old fear there…fear that the words might get jumbled…might not come out right…

VICTOR: Yes…and when I get like that…self-conscious and awkward like I used to…nothing comes out right…

THERAPIST: So it's two things again…an old part…really a younger one… that remembers all that self-consciousness and awkwardness, and you, now…who doesn't do that anymore…

Note: The therapist is attempting to make a separation between he (the adult-part) now, who doesn't stutter from the part that feels awkward.

VICTOR: It's so true…I'm like two people…*I* don't stutter any more…but *he* does!

THERAPIST: Can you ask that part…what he might need from you…some way you might be able to help him…

VICTOR: He says he wants me to trust him...he says I treat him as if he was stupid… but he isn't stupid...he's really smart…and he knows what he means.

THERAPIST: So he really wants you to trust him…he wants you to let him know that you think he's smart…

VICTOR: (very saddened) I'm awful to him sometimes...just awful…

THERAPIST: Would it be right to say…that the Critic is awful to him…but you're not…

VICTOR: Yeah…I like that…the Critic is mean…but I'm a nice guy!

THERAPIST: Yes, you are a nice guy. So as the nice guy can you ask him…if you were trusting him more...listening to him more and… treating him as if he was smart…what he thinks might happen?

VICTOR: He says the words would come out the way I want them to…he says it's me who makes him such a bad communicator…I'm the one who makes him feel so stupid…

THERAPIST: (trying to circumvent the Critic and stay focused on the positive): So he says that the words would come out right if…

VICTOR: I stay close to him…take care of him…

THERAPIST: Maybe…see what happens if you just stay close to him now…tell him that you would like things between you to change…that you want to be in a good relationship with him…

VICTOR: He wants that that a lot…and (smiles)…so do I!

The **value** of this approach is that:

- ◊ it teaches clients how to communicate with their various inner parts
- ◊ the client learns how to hear and recognize the voice, sound, tone, and quality of the parts and the Self
- ◊ the client experiences a strong sense of empowerment: the client knows the way, and the next right steps to take along the way
- ◊ the client learns empathy and acceptance
- ◊ the client begins to appreciate the value of taking the time (for which we don't usually make time) for the various parts to emerge, have a voice, and express feelings
- ◊ it teaches clients how to name the parts and integrate them, creating a sense of inner wholeness

Solution

The Solution Oriented model with its emphasis on interaction tends to *externalize* the dialogue (White, 1986). For example, if a couple is not getting along, the therapist makes *the relationship* the problem rather than the people who are in the relationship. Further, the questions being asked by the therapist take into account the interactive element, that is, how each person's actions affect the other's behavior, even if only one of them is in the room, as demonstrated in the following case.

Before considering Bob's case, here is a brief excerpt from a session with his wife, Irene. As with all couples, Bob and Irene each have their own side of the story.

Irene's side is that she wants more attention, she wants more emotional support; she wants to feel valued for all she does.

THERAPIST: So if your husband was here with us now, what do you imagine he might say?

IRENE: He would say that he feels that I'm not supportive enough of him.

THERAPIST: So he would say he wants more support from you…

IRENE: Yes…he'd say I'm not really getting what a difficult period this is for him.

THERAPIST: He's going through a difficult period…and he want you to understand that more…Suppose you asked him what kind of difference it would make to him if you were more supportive?

IRENE: He'd say he wouldn't avoid me so much…and would be more attentive. (The presenting problem in the first place!)

Now here's Bob's side of the story.

Bob is 40 years old. He feels pressured and somewhat overwhelmed as the sole supporter of his family. Irene is home with three young children, ranging from 6 months to 5 years old. Since the last child was born he is working impossibly long hours developing his own small business, and trying to make ends meet. His stress level is high, and his tolerance for most anything is low.

This is the first session. He has poured out his story and is clearly in need of some emotional support and empathy (which he doesn't feel he gets from his wife). The therapist has fully heard Bob's story, and he feels safe and understood by the therapist.

Notice how Bob is coached by the therapist to speak with and for Irene, even though she is not in the room.

THERAPIST: So let's pretend that Irene is here with us, right now. She's sitting (points) right there on the couch next to you…OK? (he nods) and I'm wondering if you'd mind if I asked her a few questions (he nods in agreement).

THERAPIST: (turns her chair a bit): Hello, Irene…I'm just wondering how you see all of this?

BOB: She'd say that I'm too self absorbed.

THERAPIST: Really…

BOB: She'd say that I'm a workaholic, that I'm out of touch with her and her concerns…and that she feels like a single parent.

THERAPIST: I see…

BOB: She'd say that I don't give our relationship any attention, that I don't take enough interest in the kids…but you see…

Right here Bob loses Irene's voice and starts to protest and justify his side of the story.

THERAPIST: (gently interrupts him) I know it is terribly hard for you, and the pressure is tremendous...but just for a moment…if it's alright…I want to ask Irene a few more questions...that might help.

BOB (relaxes): OK…

THERAPIST: Irene, let me ask you something...Is there anything that Bob can do… just one small thing…that will make a real difference for you?

BOB (settles back into Irene's voice): She'd say that she would want me to phone her a few times during the day...and especially at the end of the day when I'm leaving...in case she wants me to pick up something up on the way home.

He concedes here that he used to phone her regularly to check-in, but recently, in the past few months, has stopped doing that for lack of time.

THERAPIST: Irene, can you tell Bob…how it will be helpful to you…when he's phoning you more often.

BOB: She'd say that it would make her feel more cared about and loved…she says she feels isolated with the kids…sort of…abandoned…

THERAPIST (to Irene): Can you tell him...when you are feeling loved and cared about…how that changes things for you?

BOB: She'd say that she'd be more tolerant and understanding…she'd say she appreciates how much I've got on my plate…she'd say she wouldn't nag me so much.

THERAPIST (turns back toward Bob): So when she's tolerant and understanding… and not nagging…how will that change things for you?

BOB: I guess I'd want to spend more time at home...and be more attentive to her. (The presenting problem!)

Notice how masterfully the Solution Oriented model uses language to gently "weave" (Insoo Kim Berg's coinage) the points of view of each side into the creation of the Solution Picture. The therapist shuttles back and forth, carefully noticing what she would say, what he would say, while constantly observing how each new alteration in action and behavior will affect the other - an essential component of this model. The client eventually arrives, often seemingly magically, at an "Aha!" place, which leads in turn to an appropriate action step.

The **value** in this approach is that:

◊ The client gets a better understanding about the nature of an interaction, and how what he or she says and does impacts upon others.

◊ The model points clients toward new patterns of behavior, and helps them move toward altering dysfunctional interactions.

◊ The questions are structured to include both parties; therefore, the therapist has the option of working on the relationship (even with entire families) with only one party present.

◊ The client learns listening skills and consideration by modeling (rather than teaching). Through the process of speaking for the "other side" the client becomes more aware and begins to see the bigger picture.

Note: Brief therapists often refer to the style of questioning above as *circular questioning.* However, it should be noted for the sake of accuracy that the actual practice was developed in Italy by the Milan Team, to address the issues of working with rigid family systems. The intent was to introduce, as Gregory Bateson would say, *news of a difference* into the family's thought-process (and hence the system) by having members "gossip in the presence" of each other. The process above resembles circular questioning, but has a more collaborative purpose.

INTEGRATION SPOT

Experiential *listening* is at the core of the Focusing Oriented model. The skillful use of asking *questions* is at the core of the Solution Oriented model. Both models use listening as a way of helping clients feel valued and understood.

The Focusing model has developed the skill of listening into a highly refined art form. The Solution model would be deeply enriched by adding fragments of *experiential listening* to its approach. The two models can be easily combined.

INTEGRATION: *Asking* Solution Oriented questions using the Focusing Oriented approach to *listening.* For example:

Therapist (*asks* in Solution style): If she was here with you, right now... what do you imagine she'd say you could do, that would be helpful to her?

Client: She'd say she wants me to phone her more often.

Therapist (*listens* and *reflects* in Focusing style): So, she says, that your calling her more often would make a real difference to her...

Client (takes a moment to *experience* what the therapist has said): Yes, it would help her feel more appreciated...

Therapist (*listens* and *reflects* in Focusing style): She will feel more appreciated by you...

CLIENT (*experiences*): Yes…she really would.

THERAPIST (*asks* in Solution style): How do you imagine it will be for you…when she's feeling more appreciated?

CLIENT: She'll be so much more understanding about what's going on for me…

THERAPIST (*listens* and *reflects* in Focusing style): You'll feel so much more understood by her…you feel she'll understand so much more about…what a stressful period this is for you…

CLIENT (*experiences*): Yes..I know she would…and that would be such a relief…to feel that we were really on the same side…

Solution: Concentrates on, What will *be* different?

Focusing: Concentrates on, What will *feel* different?

The *SOFT* approach combines both models.

Conjoint Sessions: The Fine Art of Relating Interactively

People generally quarrel because they cannot argue.

Gilbert K. Chesterton

As all skilled therapists know, working with two people, whether they are couples, siblings, parent and child, or any other configuration, can be more than challenging.

When the two people in the room are both committed to making change together, it is not an overstatement to say this is "heaven" for the therapist. When, however, the two people are in major conflict, can't listen, and attack each other mercilessly, it is also not an overstatement to say that these sessions can be "hell" for the therapist, reducing him/her (especially if the session begins to spin out of control) to feeling something like a referee.

The Both/And Approach To Therapy

Generally, the Brief Therapy models are the best suited to dealing with "impossible" couples. The language is specific, stays focused on goals, looks for positive next steps, and adroitly circumvents "the problem" by concentrating on "the solution" (proposed by the clients).

What does not get addressed however, is the intense and very real feelings that build up between people during the course of a long term relationship - whether it be with couples, members of a family, or any other groups. (From this point on I will use the word "couple" to denote any two people). The parties involved do get *relief* from the problem, but they do not necessarily get *heard* in their deep core places where, in Focusing language, they "carry the problem." In fairness to Brief Therapy, the deep hearing of feelings was never meant to be the goal, or even part of the equation, so the Brief models should not be derided for the omission.

Because the Focusing Oriented therapist is highly skilled in Experiential Listening, and further, because the Focusing approach was developed to help clients explore their "inner process" in the first place, the idea of avoiding listening to a client's feelings is tantamount to sacrilege.

This is the juncture where we need to consider a both/and approach.

In the case of a difficult couple, for example, the Solution approach is ideal to keep the session progressing smoothly. But there comes a point in a relationship where the parties involved need to learn how to listen to each other, if not with agreement, then at least with respect and tolerance.

A Paradox:

Brief Therapy

The purpose of all Brief approaches is to get clients functioning well, as quickly as possible, outside of the therapy room. Using skillfully worded questions, the Brief Therapy models work superbly in managing difficult couples in the room. However, when the couple leaves the session they don't always have the skills to stay focused on the positive, or see the circularity of their behavior. The clients' lack of skills is further exacerbated by the fact that psycho-education is not generally a component of the Brief Therapy approaches.

Experiential Therapy

Because of their intrapsychic orientation, Experiential models do not always lend themselves to questioning couples as skillfully as their Brief counterparts. In the worst-case scenario, the Experiential therapist can lose control of the session by allowing too much feeling (if there is such a concept) to emerge in the course of an hour. However, the Focusing Oriented therapist is usually a very skilled teacher; and psycho-education is part and parcel of the Focusing process. The therapist often teaches the clients some very specific relational skills. Therefore, clients tend to leave the session with very clear ground-rules outlining how, in measured turns, they can listen more effectively to each other.

We are back to a both/and approach.

The Interactive Focusing Process

To listen well is as powerful a means of influence as to talk well.

Plutarch

The Focusing process, in both its original 6-step form, and later as a model of therapy, was designed to help individuals learn more about themselves and deepen their inner experience. The Focusing process never addressed (nor was it designed to) the needs of couples and families.

Just as Brief Therapy has evolved and changed over the years, and continues to do so, the process of adapting a Focusing Orientation to therapy has as well, and continues to go through its own ongoing evolution. In the 1980's Janet Klein, Psy. D., a long time member of the Focusing community, saw a need to expand the way Focusing was utilized to include the needs of people struggling with relational issues. She developed a model called the *Interactive Focusing Process* (Klein, 1999). The model, which she developed with Dr. Mary McGuire, included the basic components of Focusing: listening, empathy, respectful attitude, and monitoring the felt-sense; but for the first time, the model was applied interactively.[†]

Part of the success of the Solution Oriented approach is based on the therapist's *skill in asking questions.* The success of the Interactive approach is based on the *skill of listening* - not of the therapist to the client, but rather, of how clients listen to each other.

Note: The following explanations and ground-rules for Interactive Listening may seem, at first glance, foreign to those practicing Brief Therapy: First, because the explanations involve a fair bit of teaching and time (a notion that is antithetical to being brief) and second, because the process is very affect-oriented (and although that is changing somewhat in the Brief world, according to the original models, it is still something akin to "uncommon therapy"!)

† Les Greenberg, a colleague of Eugene Gendlin, developed with Sue Johnson his own approach to *Facilitating Emotional Change* (Greenberg *et al.*, 1993) with couples using their model, *Emotionally Focused Therapy* (Greenberg & Johnson, 1988).

Note: Keep in mind that the structure of the Interactive Focusing Process does not need to be implemented in its entirety. This book is about integrating parts of models that clinicians feel will enhance their work and expand their therapeutic options. I encourage those practicing Brief Therapy to do the Experiential thing - *sit with it!*

The Framework for Getting Started

To begin, I suggest the following to clients in bits and pieces over time. The purpose of these points is to normalize the process of disagreeing:

◊ We get along with some people some of the time. We don't get along with some people, even those we care deeply about, some of the time.

◊ We are conditioned to believe that not getting along, disagreeing, arguing, or dissention of any sort is somehow bad, not adult, and should be avoided at all costs. This is a problem! Not the disagreeing part, but rather the belief - the false belief - that not getting along at times is a negative thing.

◊ Disagreeing is natural and normal. Learning how to *manage* disagreeing is a real form of creativity, and a way to grow with a partner at a new level of being and awareness.

◊ Knowing how to be with someone in a conflictual situation requires some skill and some ground-rules, so that interaction can take place within a framework that encourages a successful dialogue.

What is needed to begin the Interactive Focusing Process:

◊ A space between two or more people in which a shared experience happens, and in which all parties are equally heard.

◊ A way of relating where the parties involved are able to maintain some sense of Self and composure (while the intensity of the issue is still manageable): the difference between interactional and confrontational.

◊ A desire to communicate: willingness to listen openly to issues that generate feelings of discomfort, disagreement, or the unease connected with misunderstanding.

BOUNDARIES: Staying Protected and Connected

In order to have successful interactions with anyone, whether it be a partner/ spouse, colleague, friend, relative or child, we need to have some understanding of boundaries: what they are, what they do, and how they flex and bend (or not) with different individuals at different times (or even with the same individual in any given moment!)

The poet, Robert Frost wisely said, "Good fences make good neighbors." While I love this expression, I am also keenly aware that for some, this quote creates a feeling of safety and security, and for others a definite feeling of being excluded or left out.

When reflecting on boundaries (whether they are physical, emotional, mental, psychological, or spiritual) a number of questions arise: How do we assess what kind of boundaries we want and need – and in what circumstances?

- ◊ What do we want to let in?
- ◊ What do we want to keep out?
- ◊ What do we feel we need to protect?
- ◊ What do we feel we want to share?

These questions awaken some interesting considerations. To begin, what *exactly* is a boundary? Webster's Dictionary defines it as: "a border, limit, dividing line, or barrier." These words, however, have little psychological meaning unless we add the component of *personal perception* in relation to *direct experience* - which is of course, varied. It is the subjective experience that determines where we draw our "lines in the sand", so to speak. For example, for one who has been physically abused, the sexual boundary will be quite different, and perhaps more hard or solid, than for the person who has not had such a traumatic experience. For the latter person, the softer term "setting limits" may suffice quite well.

We all know that there are times to say *'no'* and times to say *'yes'*. What we are exploring here is what determines where, when, and how we draw the line – and how to know. Sometimes those definitions are clear; other times they are more vague. Sometimes we need time and space to sort out what feels like the appropriate boundary, and after consideration, arrive at a more *elastic* solution: with one particular person the answer is *'yes'*, with another it is *'no'*. In other instances we make our decisions conditional upon 'something': *"I'll say 'yes' under these circumstances."*

Another consideration is texture. *What is a personal boundary made of?* In psychology, we talk about *hard* and *soft* boundaries, and *flexible* or *inflexible* boundaries.

For example, consider the word 'hard' (as in having a *hard boundary*). Initially *hard* doesn't have a welcoming ring to it: *"I don't want to be hard."* However, if we apply that word to the perpetration of abuse (in any form), we would be inclined to say that we have a clear-cut *hard boundary* regarding abusive behavior: It is not OK – ever!

And, while being 'soft' initially sounds more flexible and welcoming, if someone is continually abusive to you (at any level) having a *soft boundary* is inappropriate.

Each individual has his/her own personal limits, tolerances, and particular spots where s/he has to "draw the line".

Example: Teenagers generally have a much higher tolerance for loud music than most adults. Therefore, the limit of what a parent might be able to tolerate in noise levels will be quite different than what a group of teens having a party can tolerate.

The Point: How we each draw our lines marking where we say *'yes'* and *'no'* is colored by personal experience and *felt-memory:* the mind says, *"It's really OK this time..."* and the body says, *"No way...I've been here before!"*

Therefore, it might be right to say that we have a myriad of boundaries made of various (inner) substances from hard like armor, to soft like a gauze cloth. Each individual will most likely have to assess and re-invent, freshly, with his or her own subjective set of rules, from relationship to relationship, *what feels right, right now.*

INNER AND OUTER BOUNDARIES

We have already determined that there are different types, textures, and perceptions regarding boundaries. There are also different uses for boundaries. Using the example of "good fences", a boundary can be used in two ways: to *keep something out* or to *keep something in* - as in 'contained'. When we talk about personal boundaries we often refer to them as being *external* or *internal.*

External Boundaries:

An *external boundary* includes physical space, proximity to others, and what you will or will not let in:

◊ How close (or far) you want to be with people in a physical space.

◊ Your comfort level with touching: hugs, kisses, putting an arm around you, or where a person will stand or sit in relation to you.

  (Note: Have you ever gone to hug someone and they immediately put out their hand for a shake, instead? It is essential to recognize the difference between what feels OK and normal for us, and what seems normal to another, and whether those differences are personal or cultural.)

◊ Your privacy comfort level: Is it OK for someone to go through your drawers? Read your mail? Listen in on a phone conversation? How private do you feel you need to be for comfort and safety?

◊ Maintaining safe sexual boundaries: You have a right to say *'no'*.

  (Note: A person who 'acts out', threatens, pouts, mopes, and doesn't respect your right to say *'no'* is committing a serious *boundary violation.*)

Internal Boundaries:

An *internal boundary* is the limit that we draw regarding where we end, and someone else begins. Noted author, Terry Real, has a wonderful explanation for the internal boundary. He says, *"The internal boundary is to your psyche like your skin is to your body."* He also talks about the internal boundary as having two dimensions: the *containing boundary* and the *protective boundary*.

The *containing boundary* relates to your ability to refrain from "spilling" your inner feelings on to others when you are feeling out of sorts, angry, not your self, or out of control. Spilling anger, rage, moodiness, self-pity, or any other negative behavior on to others is not only a *boundary violation*, it is as spiritually and psychologically illegal as spilling an actual toxic substance (like acid) on to another person. A well-functioning *containing boundary* allows us to maintain a safe and self-nurturing space for ourselves, without contaminating others with toxic emotional spills.

Here is a visual picture to consider:

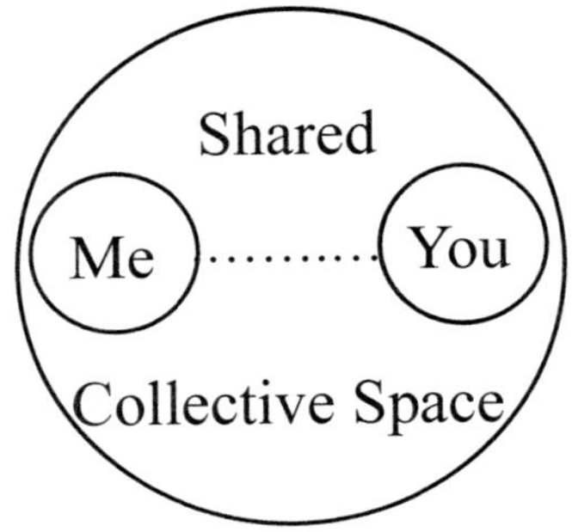

We have a large circle, which represents the collective *us* or *we.* Within the circle there are two containers of equal size, representing two individuals: *me* and *you.* Notice the line indicates that we are connected yet separate. There is plenty of space in the large circle for both containers (*me* and *you*) to exist peacefully. The contents in each container, however, must remain *contained* within the container (especially if the container is filled with anger, rage, and negative feelings). A *boundary violation* means spilling what is in your container into either the other person's container, or into the collective shared space.

The *protective boundary* relates to keeping the 'I' or adult-self undamaged and intact when someone is negative, judgmental, harsh, or hurtful toward us. When the *protective boundary* is whole and functioning, we are able to make a separation between 'I' and 'other'.

We can acknowledge that someone else feels as they do, and/also, we have the right to agree or disagree with another's point of view about us, hopefully with a *right attitude: "We're not always in agreement, but I still respect and value you."*

Note: If we allude back to the work on the Critic, it is clear that when someone accuses us of something, (just like the Critic) the message is *partially right.* The problem is that we can't hear what someone is saying, or learn from it, because the other's evaluation is not clothed as *constructive feed-back* (with *right attitude*) but rather judgment, criticism or blame. Notice the difference between:

- *"You are so selfish."* vs. *"I wish you would share more openly."*

- *"You don't know what you're talking about."* vs. *"I have a different view of that than you do."*

- *"You always do that."* vs. *"I have a real problem when that happens."*

A good, functioning *protective boundary* allows us to say, "I *get* that you are very mad at me right now…" without crumbling or attacking back. The protective boundary is what allows a person to remain *connected* yet *protected*, in conflictual situations.

WHEN BOUNDARIES AREN'T WORKING

Boundary Failure: Boundaries can break down for a number of reasons:

◊ Fear of being disliked: A person is needy, too emotionally attached, fearful of being rejected, fearful of hurting another.

◊ The boundary between Self and other is dysfunctional: There is confusion between empathy and identification: Someone else's feelings become your feelings; their pain becomes your pain; their frustration and anxiety becomes your frustration and anxiety. What someone else negatively feels (either about themselves, or critically about you) goes straight through the heart or gut, with no boundary protection.

◊ Lack of safety: The person is fearful of retribution, or getting hurt, and therefore has to be compliant. (This is a very unsafe circumstance.)

Boundary Rigidity: The opposite of boundary failure is boundary rigidity. The person is too walled-off, too emotionally withdrawn, or as we say in Focusing, "too distant". In this scenario:

◊ The person is unable to empathize: The heart is blocked, usually from fear of getting hurt – again.

◊ Retraumatization: The person is fearful of having old wounds reopened and getting "triggered". The dysfunctional solution becomes minimizing the other person's feelings in order to minimize one's own (pain).

◊ Negative Beliefs: showing or demonstrating feeling states will be viewed as a sign of weakness:

- *Don't be a crybaby.*
- *Who says life is fair?*
- *How can you complain when people in...*(name any Third World country) *are starving?*
- *Don't be a wimp. Stop complaining and get on with it!*
- *Real men don't cry.*

The walled-off individual has *inflexible boundaries*. Complicating the situation is the fact that s/he is generally pleased to be this way. The person who is distant, unfeeling, and walled-off often has no motivation to change. It feels good not to feel; it feels good to be separated from the pain. Sometimes the person even feels a sense of pride about not feeling - a sense of grandiosity and arrogance about not succumbing to (mere) 'emotionality'.

HEALING

The work of healing relationships requires clear and reasonable boundaries for both parties.

Having healthy boundaries requires thought, flexibility, and the wisdom to know when to say *'yes'* and when to say *'no'*. When boundaries are working properly, saying *'no'* feels right, and (in many cases) feels as good as saying *'yes'*.

◊ **Soft Boundaries:** Knowing how to say 'no', with grace, caring, empathy, and understanding toward the other.

◊ **Hard Boundaries:** Knowing how to say 'no', clearly, firmly, and respectfully, making I-statements rather than you-statements:

- *"This is not right for me."* vs. *"You don't know what you're talking about."*

- *"I'm sorry, but I'm just not comfortable with it. I'll have to say 'no'"* vs. *"Are you crazy? That's the stupidest idea I've ever heard!"*

◊ **Flexible Boundaries:** You are open to negotiation, change, and re-setting reasonable new limits. You have an 'attitude' that suggests willingness and pliability, but not giving the impression that you will have your boundaries violated in any way, either.

If a person is critical, judgmental, name-calling, yelling, etc., there is a *right process* involved for getting back into alignment, both with one's self, and with another:

◊ First, is having a clear *protective boundary*: This keeps the other's words and actions from piercing or damaging the Self. In this introverted state, self-nurturing, self-protection and keeping oneself safe, is the key.

◊ Second, is the ability to *make clear distinctions*:

- *This is how it is for them* (other).
- *This is NOT how it is for me.*

◊ Third, knowing how to make a boundary that has simultaneously, both *hard and soft components* to it, for example, a wall with a door or window in it. (Use any visual images that work for you.)

If someone throws something at your wall (boundary) you stop and ask yourself:

- *Is there any truth in this for me?*
- *Is what the other is saying even partially right?*

If it is untrue, let the comment slide off the wall (as T. Real says) "like a raw egg". If it is true – even partially true, allow the door (or window) to open a bit, take it in, *sit with it* over time, then ask yourself, *"Is this worth paying attention to?...changing?"* – NOT in order to placate the other person, but because making the change *"will make me a better person."*

Example: Your partner says that you are withdrawn and moody. Instead of reacting, *"No, I'm not, you're just a pain in the neck!"* you ask yourself, *"Is it true?" "Do I withdraw?" "Am I overly moody?"*

If there is truth in it, then taking responsibility for making the change, becoming more open, more forthcoming, and more connected, will not only feel better (and make a better relationship), it will re-align the energy from a false defensive boundary, *"Get away from me"*, to a functional *protective* boundary *"I'm not in a place to talk about it now, but how about this evening...if that works for you."*

In closing, we are all relational beings. We are required, unless we are living as hermits, to interact with other people at various levels of connection and intimacy. The quality of our relationships is dependent upon the quality of our boundaries.

Healthy relationships require healthy boundaries. †

---

† This work has been adapted from the work of Terry Real: *I Don't Want To Talk About It* (1997) and *How Can I Get Through To You* (2002).

Ground-rules for Successful Interactions

The following ground-rules can be taught verbally by the therapist, given as written hand-outs at the end of the session, or both. Clients are encouraged to study and practice between sessions.

- ◊ **Attitude:** Maintain an attitude toward the other that includes non-judgment, empathy, safety, presentness, listening, and valuing the right of the other to feel what they feel, think what they think, and be who they are. This can be summed up by the term unconditional positive regard toward the Self and others.

- ◊ **Monitoring one's bodily felt-sense:**Staying in touch with and trusting the inner sense of knowing - what feels right in any given moment.

- ◊ **Context vs. Content:** Protect the space of context: how we are with each other. The relationship is more important than being right, winning, or getting one's own way. The message is: I may not agree with you, but you still have value to me as a person. Content is the stuff that we are not agreeing about right now. In a contextual space we can still maintain a sense of connectedness with another.

- ◊ **Experiencing someone else's truth:** In conflictual situations we often feel certain that we know what the other is thinking and feeling. This is called projection and has nothing whatsoever to do with truth. (With right attitude as implicit) we need to understand how the other carries the issue inside: "How is this for you, right now?" It is impossible for us to experience caring and empathy unless we can fully grasp how an issue sits inside the other. Note: this is different than feeling that I have to agree with you. That is content. Context involves caring about the other's point of view and their right to have it, whether I agree with it or not.

- ◊ **Safety:** Joint agreement not to quit, walk out, bolt, withdraw, be destructive, or use against you information that you have previously shared. If a stalemate occurs, e.g., I can't listen anymore, you can agree to stop and continue in another session at another time. An atmosphere of safety is essential in order for people to open up and genuinely express themselves.

Listening Interactively

Essential to successful communication and supportive relationships is the ability to listen. Therapists are used to listening; it is part of their training. Clients are used to being listened to by their therapists; they take it for granted. What is new for clients is the practice of *learning how to listen to each other!* The therapist coaches the client in the two models below, *Experiential Listening* and/or *Interactive Listening* (with practice they can be done simultaneously). Clients eventually reach a point where they can listen to each other independently of the therapist.

1. **Experiential Listening:** The listener reflects back, from his/her own felt-sense, what the speaker has said; i.e., what the listener *senses* the speaker *means*, without adding any personal opinions, feelings, or advice. This type of listening simply requires the listener to *be with* the speaker, fully taking in what the speaker is saying in order to help the speaker get in touch with and clarify his/her own unique feelings.

2. **Interactive Listening:** The listener *takes in* what the speaker has said, reflects it back for accuracy, and then responds by telling the speaker how that "*sits inside of me*." (This model will be explained more fully later on.)

Listening to someone else is a relatively easy skill to learn. Listening to someone else whose problem is *you* is slightly more complex and requires using both a *protective boundary:* to keep an inner feeling of safety, and maintaining a *containing boundary:* to be able to listen without reacting.

If listening from the felt-sense is new for the client, an effective way to teach Experiential Listening (the easiest of the two models) is by using the following 3-step format:

Step 1: The listener responds to what the speaker has said:

> *What I understand you mean is...*
> *It sounds like you're saying...*
> *What you're saying is...*
> *It seems like...*
> *You're saying that...*

Or, the listener can simply reflect back what the speaker has said without any preface.

Correct:

> HE: *I'm really mad that you were late.*
>
> SHE: *You're feeling really mad at me for being late.*

The listener learns how to say back what s/he understands is the crux of what the speaker is *saying* and *meaning* - NOT the listener's interpretation or reaction:

Incorrect:

> HE: *I'm really mad that you were late.*
>
> SHE: *There you go again, blaming me for everything...without even asking me why I was late!*

Here we have a *reaction,* instead of a *response.* The listener has lost her *containing boundary.*

Step 2: The listener checks with the speaker to make sure that s/he has heard the speaker correctly:

> *Have I got that right?* or *Did I get it the way you meant it?*

If the speaker has already said, "That's *exactly* what I mean!", then this step is redundant. If the speaker is hesitant, "Well…that's *sort of* what I mean…", then the listener makes a revision, "So that's *not quite right*…Can you say it again?"

Step 3: The listener invites the speaker to continue:

> *Is there more...?*
>
> *Maybe see if there's anything else...about that...*

These simple words invite the speaker to go more deeply into the issue. The speaker continues until he reaches a point where he feels heard and understood. Then the two people switch roles. The original speaker is now the listener, and generally feels good about being the listener, because he has been heard. The original listener is now inclined to speak from a more present and less reactive space; she now has a much better understanding about how her partner feels. She may have her own upsets, but is less likely to be reactive.

Comments:

For the clients: Something profoundly transformative happens when two people in conflict finally *hear* and *grasp* (often for the first time in a long time) what the other is actually feeling, holding, and carrying inside – with both empathy and understanding.

For the therapist: Knowing that you have facilitated the beginning of a new level of harmony, as you watch two people communicating and connecting more effectively (often for the first time in a long time) is equally inspiring.

The Difference Between Unsafe and Uncomfortable

The process of therapy is safe; it is not always comfortable. The process (between couples) outside of the therapy room should follow suit - maybe not comfortable but always safe.

Uncomfortable: Uneasy, off-balance, a definite *felt* experience of not-rightness. By maintaining the *Focusing Attitude* clients can begin to learn from these off-balance feelings; they learn how to sit with them and keep them company. It often feels scary and safe at the same time (like a roller coaster ride). The experience is tolerable/bearable, and intrinsic to expanding awareness and understanding.

Unsafe: Intolerable, unbearable, a definite *felt* experience of danger, smothering, no air, or death. Unsafe is not only intolerable and unacceptable (in both interaction with others, and with ourselves, e.g. a Critic attack), feeling unsafe is a violation of the core Self. Anything that violates the Self, externally or internally, should be considered immoral and illegal - in both a physical and psychological/spiritual sense.

Note: It is easy to teach clients how to experience the difference between unsafe and uncomfortable: Ask them to recall various situations in their lives, both positive and negative, noticing how the felt-sense shifts in their bodies, when it *feels OK*, and when it feels *not OK*. The awareness will help them to keep their sense of Self in a relationship.

Contextual responses: Teach clients first how to monitor and stay with a felt-sense of danger, and second, how to use language more constructively, so they can avoid getting hooked into negative dialogue. For example, if the client is interacting with an accusing or unsafe-feeling person, some *contextual* responses might be:

I would really like to work this out with you and...

◊ *Our connection isn't quite right here...maybe you can say more about where you are right now...*

◊ *We were really working this through quite well before, but something has gone off track...do you sense that as well?*

◊ *I know that you are trying to communicate something that is very important to you, but I am unable to hear it the way you are saying it right now.*

These examples take the interaction out of *content* and place it back in *context*. (Interactions become unsafe when we get stuck in content.)

Staying in Context during an External Attack:

In an interaction, if the speaker is critical of the listener, it is essential that the therapist teaches the listener how to protect his/her inner safety.

◊ Only *reflect* what the speaker is saying.

◊ Avoid *content*, explanations, and justifications.

◊ Avoid answering direct questions - they are probably loaded!

Example:

MOTHER: If you were a good daughter like Rosie, you'd come to see me more often…you don't care what happens to me…

DAUGHTER (responding contextually): It sounds like you're disappointed that I don't get here more often.

MOTHER: Wouldn't you be…? I sit here day after day…I need help with shopping…so what's a daughter for?…All the things I used to do for you…

DAUGHTER: I hear you Mom, and I hear your loneliness and frustration.

The daughter stays with the *meaning* underlying the words.

MOTHER : So…why don't you come more often if you're so understanding?

This is a trap: No content, no justification, no excuse, will satisfy this mother. Notice how the daughter keeps her own space safe.

DAUGHTER: Mom, no matter what I say about why I can't come more often than I do…even if it was the best excuse in the world…I really don't believe that it would satisfy you. (Contextual statement) I hear that you are disappointed with me as a daughter…That must be hard for you…that I'm not like Rosie.

MOTHER: That's not true at all…I'm not disappointed with you…How could you say such a thing!...I'm just lonely, that's all…I need more company.

The real context, *I'm lonely,* has now emerged. Notice how different that is from the content, *You're not a good daughter.* The daughter can now reflect more accurately what she *senses* her mother *means.*

DAUGHTER: It's really tough, having lost so many of your friends...you had some fun times with those people in the old days…

MOTHER: Yeah…Remember Margaret? Did I ever tell you about the time we sneaked out of the house in disguise and had a crazy night on the town?

DAUGHTER: I want to hear all about it…let me pour us some tea…and I brought you some cookies…

It takes some strategy and energy to deal with critical people. Some helpful pointers to teach clients:

◊ Be a good listener.

◊ Keep the attention focused on the critical person. (In all probability they feel *unheard* anyway, and need to talk.)

◊ Avoid trying to make yourself heard or understood.

◊ Avoid looking to critical people for approval.

◊ Be as empathic as you can. (It will feel better to you, and to the other person.)

◊ Acknowledge to yourself that this relationship may be one-sided and may continue to be. Make peace with it!

◊ Find a caring, healing person to listen to you after an interaction with a critical person.

Effective Interactions Require:

◊ Honesty: say what is true and real in the moment.

◊ Ownership: I-statements; this is how I feel (we don't need to agree.)

I-statements are quite different from *you-statements* that point a finger, accuse, blame, or make make the other person wrong. They did what they did and *I feel this way about it.*

◊ Describe what happened: "This happened" rather than "when you did this, it made me feel". Notice how the "when you did this" ascribes subtle blame or intention of wrong-doing to the other.

◊ Speak in the present (also called "monitoring" the felt-sense): "How does it feel in me freshly, *right now"?* This is very different than the memory of how it felt, yesterday.

◊ Take TIME-OUT: In general, each individual has a different level of tolerance for working out conflictual situations and unpleasantness. Some people thrive on the energy of a disagreement. Others will avoid it at all costs.

Note: *A professional already has these skills but the client doesn't!*

Couples need to be taught how to:

◊ Respect time-out if the interaction is going nowhere, is too heated, or one of the parties can't listen any further.

◊ Learn tolerance for each other's ability to process difficult situations. Sometimes it is necessary for one partner to postpone a discussion until later, or tomorrow, in order to *sleep on it*. Essential to a good relationship is awareness, respect, and tolerance of a partner's capacity for processing. If necessary, take time-out, and arrange to continue at another mutually agreeable time.

Note: The couple needs to respect the commitment to meet again at the agreed upon time, otherwise one or another of the parties (usually the one that has less tolerance for confrontation in the first place) can slip into, "I'm not in the mood...maybe some other time…"

Finally, teach couples how to value the process and the efforts they are making to have more effective and rewarding interactions. Every time we manage to resolve differences in ways which allow room for each of us to *be*, respectfully, sanely, and with caring, we create a positive ripple effect for ourselves, our families, our friends, our communities, and ultimately the collective consciousness of the human family.

The Interactive Process With a Couple (Coached)

For the therapist, the initial coaching process is quite active. Over time, as clients become more familiar, comfortable and skillful with listening interactively, longer stretches of (un-coached) time will take place with less intervention from the clinician. The following examples assume familiarity with the preceding guidelines on the Interactive Focusing Process, especially the concept of *I-statements* vs. *you-statements*

Note: My rule for *you-statements* is that only complimentary ones are acceptable:

- ◊ *You are terrific.*
- ◊ *You are so funny.*
- ◊ *You are so kind.*
- ◊ *You are the best thing that has ever happened to me!*

Example (coached):

WIFE (to husband): You never listen to me…you don't respect my feelings…and have no idea where I'm coming from.

THERAPIST (gently): Can you say that in another way…using "I"?

WIFE (to husband): I don't feel heard by you…I don't feel that my feelings are respected…and sometimes I feel like you don't have a clue where I'm coming from.

THERAPIST (to him): Can you say back what you sense she meant here?

HUSBAND: Complaining, complaining...she's always criticizing me…she always makes me wrong.

THERAPIST (to him): It's clear that you have your own feelings, and I promise, we are going to hear your side of things…but just for the moment, can you say back what you think she meant…

HUSBAND: Hugghh?...I don't remember...(to wife) Can you say it again...?

WIFE: I said...I don't feel like you hear me...my side of things...I don't feel like you understand me...and I don't feel respected by you.

THERAPIST (to him): See if you can just say back what you think she *means*.

HUSBAND: She's saying that she feels that I don't understand her...that I don't respect her...and that I'm not open to her side of things.

He has said it back, but the issue is not yet internalized. Still, the therapist is encouraging.

THERAPIST: That was much better...

When couples are new to listening interactively, they will each tend to address their statements directly to the therapist because:

- ◊ Clients feel safer opening up and expressing themselves. (They perceive that even if their partner doesn't understand them at least the therapist will!)
- ◊ The therapist can coach them to speak more freely about what they are experiencing.

When couples are more comfortable and skilled with the listening process they will want to speak directly to each other (a sign to the clinician that s/he is making progress).

THERAPIST (to him): Can you say how that *makes you feel*...when your wife says that she feels so...not understood or respected...that she feels her side of things...isn't valued...?

HUSBAND: Yeah, I get that she doesn't feel good about those things.

THERAPIST: So you do understand how she feels...Now, I'm asking you something a bit more subtle here...how does it *feel to you* that she feels that way?

HUSBAND: I don't know...she always talks like that.

THERAPIST: May I ask you something? (Husband nods affirmatively.) Has there ever been anyone in your life who misunderstood you?...Where you were coming from...how you felt about things...?

The therapist is trying to get him to internalize the issue.

HUSBAND: Yeah, it was like that with my father...he was so critical...always let me know what I was doing wrong...never understood me...

THERAPIST (gently): He really never understood you...and that did *something to you inside*...Can you remember how that made you feel?

HUSBAND: It was awful really...I felt very lonely as a kid...I knew he favored my brother...and I felt sort of worthless...like nothing I said mattered.

THERAPIST: That sounds like a terrible experience...feeling so undervalued...

HUSBAND: Yes, it was...I felt very worthless and misunderstood...

THERAPIST: Those bad feelings that you're remembering, right now...what if I said that...this is a bit of how your wife is feeling...sometimes around you... just the way you described it...

HUSBAND: (horrified) Oh God!...is that how I make you feel?

WIFE: Yes...a lot of the time...

This is the first time he experiences an *empathic connection.*

HUSBAND: That makes me feel terrible...I just didn't make the connection until this minute...I really make you feel like that?

WIFE: Yes, sometimes...

HUSBAND: I'll be damned…guess you've been trying to tell me that…but I didn't want to hear you…guess I was afraid that you'd say something that would make me feel bad about myself…just like I used to with my father...wow...!

THERAPIST (to her): Can you tell him what you are experiencing, right now?

WIFE: This is the first time in many years…that I feel like you're hearing me…and it feels really good…(takes his hand)…If we could connect like this more often…I think we'd get our marriage back on track.

Comments:

For Brief Therapists: As you can see, this is a process that takes time, patience, considerable coaching, and a certain kind of tolerance for dealing with the affective components of the relationship. While many Brief therapists may not wish to embark on such a lengthy exercise in empathic Interactive Listening, teaching clients at least some of these skills can be of considerable value to them, not only outside the session, but also offering vital tools for long-term gain that will filter down into their interactions with families, and beyond…

The Interactive Process With a Couple (Not Coached)

The purpose of Interactive Listening is to:

◊ Provide a safe format in which each partner can express his/her feelings.

◊ Increase awareness for both partners by having each one experience the *other side* of the story.

◊ Help create an external experience of wholeness that reflects the inner experience of wholeness.

The following is a transcript of a couple who have been practicing the Interactive Focusing Process for some time. They are both quite adept at it; and through coaching, have reached a place where they are open and willing to listen to each other.

This example illustrates how the process can work when no intervention from the therapist is needed outside of the session.

Review:

1. The listener reflects back what the speaker has said, so that he is certain that she has been fully understood.

2. He then expresses how what she said *feels* inside of him.

3. They switch roles: the original listener becomes the speaker, and the original speaker becomes the listener.

Example (not coached):

SHE: I felt very embarrassed and humiliated when you teased me last night in front of our company.

HE: Last night, when I was cracking those jokes…you felt like I was teasing you, and it made you feel embarrassed and humiliated.

SHE: Yes...I felt like your so-called "jokes" were targeted toward me, and frankly it hurt my feelings.

He sits with this for a moment, and then expresses how what she said *feels inside of him.*

HE: I feel badly that I made you feel badly. It was never my intention to be hurtful...If what I said gave you strong feelings of embarrassment and humiliation…that really does make me feel bad.

SHE: From what you're saying, it sounds as if you didn't plan to be hurtful...and that maybe it wasn't intentional…so I'm a bit confused about why you did that…

HE: It certainly wasn't intentional…but before I say anything more about my side of it…I just want to check if there's more that you want to say…

SHE: Thank you for that…I really feel like you're with me. Of course I want to hear your side…and…I want you to know that I was very angry with you… not so much now that we're talking about it, but last night…and I guess I want you to be more aware of the impact of your words…

HE: You want me to be more aware of what I say before I say it…because my insensitivity last night really made you angry.

SHE: Yes (relaxes)…now I feel like you've got it…and I do want to hear what was going on for you.

They now switch roles.

HE: Well...this may sound weird…but I didn't think the evening was going all that well…It got really heavy for awhile when we got into all that political stuff. I guess I was trying to change the subject and lighten things up a bit… guess it wasn't all that funny, especially if you felt it was at your expense…

She sits with what he said for a moment, then expresses how what he said feels inside of her.

SHE: I'm really very touched by what you tried to do…The argument was actually getting a bit out of hand, and I too, was thinking that the evening was going in a bad direction…

HE: I was thinking that we were going into a fun, relaxed evening. Then when everything took a turn...well, I have to work with Mark, you know…and I got a bit paranoid about having to face him Monday morning…knowing that we were on opposites sides of the political fence. You know, I didn't realize it until just now, but I really did feel freaked…like, *Oh...just get me out of here!*

SHE: So the turn the evening took was really a most unexpected surprise, and you're just realizing now how freaked you felt..and the possible repercussions at work…

HE: Yes, that's it exactly…I never meant for it to spill over on to you…I guess it was my desperate attempt to be funny…trying to change the mood…

(She sits again with what he has said, and the impact on her.)

SHE: I really get the part about when something goes awry and feeling freaked… I've had that happen to me, too…I do get that your "jokes" were not intentionally aimed toward me…

HE: I am sorry…really.

SHE: Your apology is happily accepted.

HE: How about if anything like this ever happens again…I just make sure that the "joke" doesn't have anything to do with you - or us.

SHE: That sounds good to me.

This is a good example of the fruits of coaching and practice.

In the initial stages of coaching, the process can seem a bit laborious, especially for the clinician. However, when clients can internalize an issue, and empathize with a partner, friend, child, parent, or colleague, the connection and increased understanding between them is quite profound and meaningful.

The **value** in this approach is that couples can learn how to express themselves, listen, get heard, and experience empathy, without experiencing defensiveness.

While there is some added complexity in the Interactive listening model, it seems well worth the effort. The approach takes a process which was initially designed for an individual inner experience, and expands it for relational and interactional issues.

Remember: *Clients are accustomed to being listened to by a therapist. The next step is teaching them how to listen to each other, without clinical intervention.*

Review: Ground-rules for Interactive Listening

◊ Each person gets a short turn to speak; if it is too long, the listener will not have the skill level to remember and repeat it all back.

◊ The concept of *safe-space* is clearly explained: no interrupting, no blaming, no *you-statements*, only *I-statements.*

◊ The speaker expresses his/her point of view directly from the felt-sense of his/her own direct experience.

◊ The listener reflects back what the speaker has said.

◊ The speaker lets the listener know if s/he felt understood.

◊ The listener takes a moment, to check with his/her own felt-sense, then expresses how the speaker's message *felt inside* of him/her.

◊ Each person takes turns of relatively equal length.

◊ Their dialogue continues until they reach a natural stopping point, where both feel heard and understood.

◊ Each person is welcome to ask for a *time-out* if the feeling of continuing the interaction seems too hard, too contentious, or too difficult in the moment. However, the person asking for *time-out* needs to offer a viable alternative: *I need a break as I'm feeling too much anger right now. Can we sleep on it and continue again after dinner tomorrow?*

Goals

Wants awaken intellect...the keener the want, the lustier the growth.
Wendell Phillips

Another significant feature of Solution Oriented Therapy (and Brief models) is the emphasis on clearly defining current and future goals and expectations. Great care and time are taken to outline and develop manageable goals, whether for the immediate session, for the next few sessions, or for the whole course of therapy; this is not the case in Focusing Oriented Therapy (and Experiential models).

Focusing

By nature and design, the Focusing Oriented process pays more attention to the experience the client is having during the session, and less to the outcome. The act of setting a goal is relevant only as it arises naturally during the course of therapy. The client is encouraged to *sense what feels right* to speak about or address, in the moment.

As a general rule, the therapist trusts that: by following rather than leading, the process that unfolds during the session, and the consequent outcome, will help the client in a natural and organic way toward the alleviation of the presenting issue. The work, therefore, is non-directive and non-intrusive. The therapist encourages more autonomy in clients by supporting them in doing whatever they feel like doing with/during the therapy hour.

The **value** of this approach is that it puts the responsibility for the outcome of the session with the client. The result is that the client feels empowered and in charge of his or her own process. Further, there is a strong message, both implicit and explicit: Through the process of being heard and received experientially, the client will be able to intuitively navigate toward his/her own right way, discovering in the process his/her inwardly-known or next right steps (goals) to take.

The downside of this approach is the lack of a fallback position if the work is going nowhere, for example:

◊ The session is not progressing.
◊ Change is not happening.
◊ The dialogue between the therapist and client is stuck.
◊ The therapist finds him/herself covering the same old territory with the client – yet again.

At this juncture, the clinician needs to step in and *do something* - offer some skilled direction to move the process forward.

Solution

While the Solution Oriented therapist respects the client's process, s/he takes a much more active role, as well as more responsibility, for the outcome of the session. The clinician keeps the client's *stated goals* (both long and short-term) in the forefront of awareness.

This model of therapy is intentionally focused on solutions, rather than problems. The therapist's job is to *track* the process in order to make sure that the outcome of the session is consistent with the client's goals. The Solution Picture: *What it will look like when it's right – or better?* is the guiding principle/image that determines the direction of the session.

The **value** in this approach is two-fold:

First, it is extremely time efficient, and it gets to the point smoothly and clearly:

◊ *What is the issue?*
◊ *What looks like a solution?*
◊ *What will be helpful in moving toward that solution?*

Second, the emphasis is on *action steps*. The client in this model also feels empowered, but he or she will experience the full impact of feeling more-in-control when the session is over: the client leaves the session with something tangible and constructive to do. The result is that s/he feels in charge and responsible for taking the action steps and making them a reality. Again, the client receives a strong message of trust and competency.

2nd INTERVENTION ⬣ *Formula First Session Task*

(Also developed by Insoo Kim Berg and Steve de Shazer).

To assist clients in developing and achieving goals, most Brief therapists give some form of "homework" to clients on a regular basis. Generally, the homework involves a particular kind of observation task, or doing some small action step. As sessions progress, the therapist may give the client more challenging things to do:

- ◊ trying something they have never tried before
- ◊ doing something differently on certain days or times of the week
- ◊ making a particular phone call or writing a letter that is long overdue

Sometimes the homework involves making notes about particular changes that clients notice away from the session. While giving homework is not mandatory, it is an effective way to link the session to the outside world, and to practice what was covered in the session.

It is more common at the end of the first session to give a new client an *observation* task - rather than an *action* task - especially if the therapist doesn't yet know whether the client is really a "customer" for therapy.

Note: In order to assess the client's relationship with the therapist, Solution Oriented therapists often employ these distinctions:

Visitor: Someone who has been referred, is checking things out, but may not yet be sure that they want to continue or be committed.

Complainant: Someone who is asking for and wanting change - from everyone else! These clients are not yet ready to take responsibility or ownership for the "I" who makes those the changes.

Customer: A client who is ready and willing to embark upon the process of therapy.

Formula First Session Task

The therapist asks the client to observe something (related to the presenting issue) that is *working* and that he or she wants to *continue* to have happening.

Until the next scheduled session, the clients are asked to simply notice:

- ◊ What are they doing that *works?*
- ◊ What happens when they do *more* of it?
- ◊ *Who* is most affected when it works?

INTEGRATION SPOT

I like the idea of giving homework. I like the bridge that it makes between the session, life outside the session, and the next session. I like the continuity; I like *action steps;* and I like clients to have some planned time, in one form or another, to reflect upon the work that we have done together.

The Focusing Oriented practitioner does not generally ask the client to do homework. Reluctance to be "directive" is possibly one of the reasons. Another is that dynamic change tends to happen *during* the session. The clinician assumes that, if the session has been productive and has increased the client's self-awareness, the client will quite naturally reflect upon what has happened during the interval between sessions. I make no such assumptions.

INTEGRATION: Give clients some form of homework:

- ◇ **Observation tasks**: noticing something about their behavioral patterns that they would like to change; noticing what in their life works - and doesn't.

- ◇ **Doing tasks:** journaling, keeping notes about certain changes they observe; taking specific *action steps* that they feel will be helpful.

- ◇ **Recommended reading** (if they enjoy reading).

Goals or No Goals? Where are the Holes?

The issue of having a goal - or not - is of less concern to me than *what works* on any particular day with a particular client. Both models are effective, at times. The relevant questions for me are:

- ◊ What will help a client move in the direction of change?
- ◊ What will bring a new (or renewed) sense of wholeness?

There are *holes* in each model:

Focusing

Focusing Oriented therapists need, I feel, to find a new balance between *not wanting to intrude* on a client's process, and being more willing to *help clients set goals*.

For the client-centered therapist being "directive" is anathema. It is associated with taking power away from the client, and worse, giving an unspoken message to the client that the therapist knows more about a client's process than the client does.

I would like to offer the word "directionality", my *SOFT* (Solution Oriented Focusing Therapy) word for finding a balance between *action* and *non-action,* between making gentle *suggestions* and being *directive.*

The *hole* in the Focusing Oriented model would be well-filled with a bit more "directionality", and a newfound comfort zone on the part of the therapist, in giving action steps.

Solution

Conversely, the Brief and Solution Oriented practitioners would do well to find a new balance between *staying on track* with the client's stated goals, and *allowing more time* for the inner experience of the client to emerge.

Brief therapists are sometimes so cognitively and behaviorally oriented that the act of *internally processing* is left out. What is needed is more trust in the area of time: time to allow for an *inner process* to happen, and time to allow clients to *experience the feeling of congruency* between what they are saying and what they are experiencing in the moment.

The *hole* in the Solution Oriented model would be well-filled by trusting that some *experiential time* will pay off in the end for the client, and that allowing for this time will help to create a more permanent and lasting change.

Crossroads

There are specific moments where it becomes obvious to the therapist that either model can be employed - with possibly different outcomes. The clinician comes to a crossroad: that spot where the session can either take a Solution direction (setting a goal, having a plan, finding an action step) or taking a Focusing direction (being with the issue, and staying with the feelings). My strategy in these moments is to *ask the client!*

Dory: I'm really torn…there's a part of me that can't let it go…and another part that just wants to move on…

(The therapist gives the choice to the client.)

Therapist: One part of you still has so much feeling about the break-up...and the other part just wants to move on… It sounds like you could go either way here…Maybe you need to check, freshly…to see where this process wants to take you, right now.

Dory: I do want to move on…but I still feel like I need to be with the pain just for a bit longer…

Therapist: OK…so the pain is saying, *pay attention to me*… just a bit longer…

Dory: Yeah…I know what it's about, too. It's about Christmas...it's not even about him…it's about how much I'm going to miss his family. I haven't just lost a relationship…I've lost a whole family…and all the stuff that goes with it...the family dinners…the cottage in the summer…the community... Oh, Lord!…it hurts… (tears come)

THERAPIST: Yes...it really does hurt…and it is a huge loss…you were very close with the family…

DORY: I really do need to find a way to cope with this upcoming holiday…

This may be a natural juncture to move into a Solution approach.

THERAPIST: What you are *wanting* now…is a *way to cope* with the upcoming holidays.

DORY: Yes, I have to…or I'm either going to flip out, or be paralyzed by the pain…

THERAPIST: So you want to begin to build a (Solution) picture here…what it will look like when you are coping well…and what you'll be doing. Take a moment here to see…what kinds of things will fit for you, in this picture of you…managing really well…over the holidays.

DORY: The first thing is that I have to keep really busy…

THERAPIST: So being busy is the first piece...and you want to really notice what exactly "busy" means to you…rushing around?…being with a lot of people?

DORY: That's good, I'm glad you said that…No, I don't want to be rushing around like a chicken without a head…that's the last thing I want. I want to be with friends in a meaningful way…I want to accept invitations that I know will come…I might even want to plan a dinner party of my own...create my own sense of community…

The therapist will continue to help this client build a picture that:

◊ includes specific goals to help her get through the holidays

◊ feels right and manageable at every step of the way

After the client has developed a picture that looks and feels right, the therapist will use Scaling to help her construct a plan.

3rd INTERVENTION ⬣ *Scaling*

(The intervention of Scaling was developed by Ron Krall, a colleague of Berg and de Shazer, at the Brief Family Therapy Center in Milwaukee.)

The therapist proposes making a scale from one to ten. The highest number on the scale represents what is wanted, and the lowest number, what is not wanted.

The first question, *Where would you like to be on the scale?* sets up a vision for the future: what is possible.

The second question, *Where are you right now?* helps to contrast where the client is, with how the client wants to be.

The third question, *What is a small step that will bring you up a half point, or point, higher on the scale?* addresses the action step: what the client can do that is concrete and realistic.

(Case: Dory...continued)

THERAPIST: Let's break this down to see what you want to do, and in what order. Imagine that you had a scale ranging from one to ten. Ten on the scale is how you would like to be over the holidays, shall we call that "happy"? (She nods.) And one is the other end of the scale, let's call that "unhappy". Where, given the current circumstances, do you *realistically* see yourself being on the scale...over the holidays?

> Use of the word "realistically" gives needed permission to clients, to choose a number that will congruently fit for them. There are people who would not, by their very nature, ever see themselves as a ten (unless they think they *should* be), and who would be quite contented with a seven or eight. If they are depressed or have resistance to change, they may be contented with a five or six.

DORY: I think if I put my mind to organizing the holidays really well, I could see myself somewhere between a seven and an eight.

Unhappy 1________________**7**__**8**___10 Happy

THERAPIST: Sounds good…and where would you say you are, on the scale right now?

DORY: Oh, today?...I guess about a three.

Unhappy 1____**3**____________________10 Happy

THERAPIST (looks for small manageable steps): So, what do you suppose is one small thing that you can do, between now and the next time we meet, that will take you from a three to a three and a half?…maybe even a solid four… not from a three to a seven or eight… just a half step…or a step…something that will help you feel a little more hopeful about the upcoming holidays.

DORY: I need to go through my address book. I need to figure out who I want to spend time with, and who I want to avoid…memories and all that…and maybe figure out, if I was having a dinner party, who I'd want to invite.

THERAPIST: So the process of going through your address book will be helpful... And bring you to what number?

DORY: I think if I do that…really sort through the friends I want to spend some time with…I'll feel like a four…maybe even five.

THERAPIST: Sounds good, and I look forward to hearing about your progress… good luck!

Comments:

This session included elements of both the Focusing and Solution Oriented models.

Focusing: The therapist listened and reflected in a Focusing manner, taking the necessary time to let Dory sort out her feelings.

Solution: The therapist used a Solution approach, especially Scaling, to help Dory clarify her goals, and come to terms with what she felt was realistic and manageable.

CASE: MARTY

Sometimes clients are unrealistic about what they will be able to accomplish. If you are working with a client whose expectations seem unrealistic, it is useful to check with the client before labeling the scale: *What shall we call number one? What shall we call number ten?* There are certain times when it is more useful to make the distinctions black and white: "Happy-Unhappy", "Best-Worst". At other times, as in cases of depression, or where the goal initially seems insurmountable (e.g., giving up an addiction or losing a large amount of weight), it is more effective to make the terms more relative: "Better" instead of "Best", or "Happier" instead of "Happy".

The client in the following example has unrealistic expectations. The therapist has just explained the Scaling procedure to this client who is suffering from depression, and asks him where he would like to be on the scale.

MARTY: I'd be very satisfied with an eight.

Less depressed 1__________________**8**___10 More hopeful

> Given the nature of the client's current mental state the therapist suspects that an eight on the scale may be unrealistic; she will not challenge this, but will be alert to what the client sees as realistic progress.

THERAPIST: And where would you say you are, on the scale right now?

MARTY: Hmmm...I guess a two…

Less depressed 1__**2**______________________10 More hopeful

THERAPIST: So, what do you imagine is one small thing you can do, between now and the next time we meet, that will take you from a two to maybe a two and a half?...maybe even a three?…not from a two to an eight…just a half step…something that will help you feel a little less depressed and a bit more hopeful...

MARTY: I need to go back to the gym. I need start exercising again. I've been sitting around for weeks, just eating, watching TV, and vegging out…I can't bring myself to do much of anything…and I'm putting on so much weight… I know that exercising is a good place to start…and would probably put me in a better mood.

THERAPIST: OK, that does sound like a good place to start…so, *realistically*, how many times do you imagine you'll be going to the gym between now and the next time we meet?

MARTY: Ummm…five times, and I'll take the week-end off.

A client will sometimes reply without actually thinking through what s/he has said. In this case, given the length and severity of the client's depression, the therapist doesn't feel his answer is realistic. This is a perfect integration spot for the therapist to *double-check experientially*.

INTEGRATION SPOT

Ask a Solution Oriented question, with a back-up experiential question.

THERAPIST: O.K…so you know you want to exercise more…can you maybe… just take a moment here to check and see…what your *body buys*…Maybe just imagining getting dressed…taking your gym bag…going out to the driveway…getting in the car…

It doesn't take him very long to see that what he *wants* and what he's *willing* to do *don't match*.

MARTY: Well…maybe five times is a bit much. How about two times in a week?…maybe three. I think I can do that.

THERAPIST: Marty, this for you – not to please me. Take another minute to really *sense* what feels right for you…whatever *feels realistic* and *manageable* is what's right.

MARTY (nods affirmatively): I can do that…

THERAPIST: So, you're really OK with that…this agreement with your self. Two times…and if you do it three times you can consider it a bonus!

After the client agrees to an action step, it would not be unusual for the Solution Oriented therapist to develop the action step even further by checking:

◊ *What time of day?*

◊ *What days of the week?*

◊ *What type of exercise?*

◊ *Duration of exercising?*

In the above example, it was actually the *experiential step,* taking the time to *sense* what felt reasonable, which signaled to the client that five times a week for exercising was unrealistic.

In order to achieve a positive outcome, it is very useful for the therapist to take the time to check for congruency, making sure that what clients say or think they want, matches what they actually feel they can do. Once a client can get a bodily felt-sense of what feels realistic and manageable, the therapist and client can sort out the specific details. The client then leaves the session feeling motivated and uplifted by having something to do that feels realistic, as well as concrete and manageable.

For the client the act of *setting* a goal, and also taking the time to *sense the felt-rightness* of the goal, provides a much more realistic perspective - and highlights the *both/and* experience - *doing* and *feeling*.

For the therapist integrating the two models (Solution: helping the client *set* a goal, and Focusing: helping the client *sense* the goal) gives the clinician more scope to access what we might call the client's "line of least resistance" i.e., their natural way of processing. Some clients respond better to action steps and doing; other clients respond more favorably to sensing and experiencing.

Integrating the models gives more choice, to both the therapist and client.

To Feel or Not To Feel? That is the Question?

Some people carry their hearts in their heads; many carry their heads in their hearts. The difficulty is to keep them apart, and yet both actively working together.

Samuel Taylor Coleridge

At first glance, the biggest gap between Focusing Oriented and Solution Oriented Therapy is seemingly in the way each model views the use of affect. While the two models may appear (at least initially) as being at opposite ends of the spectrum, the old adage "opposites attract" couldn't be more apt. Hence (and paradoxically), this is one of the easiest areas to bridge.

The Focusing Oriented approach takes as much time as necessary for *felt experiencing* - exploring the feeling-state of the client

The Solution Oriented approach has generally (this is changing in some Brief circles) bypassed the affective component, keeping the client's attention on the *viewing* and *doing* necessary to reach the desired goal(s).

As Eric King (1998) aptly points out in *The Role of Affect and the Emotional Context in Solution-Focused Therapy,* "greater utilization of affect (grounded in bodily senses) as evoked in both client and therapist can offer valuable clues to determining focus/goal setting and thereby expedite our clinical practice." He emphasizes the significance of allowing the time and space for affect in the clinical setting as giving the therapist important clues to clients' meanings, motivation, and goals which are so central to solution-oriented practice. Furthering this integration, Lipchik (1999) and King both highlight the centrality of alliance and empathy in Brief Therapy to create a safe emotional context for change.

To clarify how each model views the use of affect in therapy, it is helpful to return to the notion of "parallel universes" or "parallel planes":

Solution work tends to be *cognitive*, using the mind to *see* new possibilities.

__Focusing__ work tends to be *kinesthetic*, using the body as a barometer to check the *level of feeling.*

Therefore, when the therapist is conversing with the client, the direction of the dialogue, and consequently the outcome, are influenced by whether the therapist has "clothed" questions in Solution language or in Focusing language. The client in turn, will process the questions and respond at whatever level is accessed in him or her (cognitive or kinesthetic).

The __Solution__ approach imagines, supposes and wonders about:

◊ What do you *imagine* will be different, when…?

◊ Do you ever *wonder about* what it will be like when...?

The __Focusing__ approach also *imagines, supposes* and *wonders about.* However, the follow-through requires taking the images down (stairs) into the body to see what the imagining *feels like:*

Solution	**Focusing**
What do you *suppose* will be happening when…?	Can you *sense* what will be happening when…?
Then what?...What else?	See it that fits for you…check and see: *Is there more?*
What will you be *doing?*	Can you sense what you'll be *feeling?*
What do you *imagine* you will *be telling* him when it is right?	Can you *sense* what you'll *feel like saying* when it is right?
What *difference* do you think these changes will *make* to your husband?	Can you sense how your husband might *feel differently* when you make these changes?
What small steps do you think you *can take* that will be helpful to you in getting some relief from this issue?	Can you *sense* what *feels like* a step you can take that will be helpful in moving you toward a feeling of relief or fresh air?

In the Focusing Oriented approach if the client says: *There is a real sinking feeling for me with this issue,* the experiential response might be:

◊ *"Can you just let that sinking feeling know that it is OK for it to be here, right now?"*

This suggestion gives the client permission to allow the felt-sense of *all about the sinking feeling* to form into whatever, or however, the body interprets and carries the sinking feeling inside. Further, while the client is exploring the *sinking feeling* the Focusing Oriented therapist will help the client identify that yes, there is a *part* that has a sinking feeling, but it's *not the whole thing*. The client can then (if s/he chooses) move toward *what feels right.*

In the Solution Oriented approach the therapist might ask:

◊ "When this sinking feeling isn't there - or is less than it is now - what do you imagine will be *happening instead?*"

This suggestion (imagining what will be happening instead) is the Solution version of finding out what *feels right* - the place where there isn't the "sinking feeling". Because this model doesn't normally address what is wrong, or in Focusing terms "what stands in the way", the Solution Oriented therapist is less inclined to dwell on the issue of parts, which brings us to another crossroads.

More Crossroads

Again, the clinician comes to a *crossroads*: the juncture where the process can take a Focusing turn (paying attention to feelings) or a Solution turn (bypassing feelings).

Solution

The starting point for the Solution Oriented therapist has traditionally been to bypass affect (although, as already stated, this is changing for many Brief therapists) by exploring the *exception to the problem:* When the client *isn't* functioning in a negative way:

> THERAPIST: When are the times you notice that the sinking feeling is less than it is now? *or* What do you imagine you will be *doing differently* when the sinking feeling is gone, and you are feeling better?

> CLIENT: When I don't have that sinking feeling I will be more productive and creative...I will start writing again.

The Solution Oriented therapist will pursue the idea of being more productive, more creative, and writing again.

Focusing

The starting point for the Focusing Oriented therapist is to acknowledge affect by allowing the client to determine where the next steps should be:

> THERAPIST: There are two things there: A part that feels like it's sinking...and another part that feels like it wants to be productive, creative...wanting to write again...Taking a moment to sense freshly, can you ask yourself: *Which of those two parts has the most energy for me right now?*

If the client chooses to move toward the positive, *I want to be more productive and creative...I want to start writing again*, the Focusing session will run parallel to a Solution session, exploring positive next steps, that *feel right*.

If however, the client says, *I want to stay with the sinking part*, the process will take a different turn, and the therapist will say something like, *Can you sense what this sinking feeling is connected to in your life right now...?*

Each model approaches affect differently:

<u>Focusing:</u> The therapist supports the client in choosing what direction *feels* like the next right step – whether it is positive or negative.

<u>Solution:</u> The therapist supports the client in choosing what the next right step *will be.*

INTEGRATION SPOT

When it comes to using affect *let the client choose*:

◊ If the client wants to move out of the sinking feeling, and into more concrete action steps, Solution Oriented questions will help the client out of the quagmire and into *what will work.*

◊ If the client feels s/he needs to spend more time with the sinking feeling, attempting to divert his/her attention may very well prove to be a band-aid instead of a cure. The sinking feeling will probably come back, unless and until it is given time, attention, empathy, and validation.

Doing What Comes Naturally

There is no right or only way to manage a therapy session. Often the direction a session takes is a hunch based on the clinician's intuition in the moment - a *therapeutic judgment call.*

Sometimes the clinician will notice a lack of congruency between what the client is saying and feeling, i.e., the client is not really experiencing what s/he is talking about. This may be the place to stop, slow down, and give the client some process time to *be with,* rather than immediately trying to *fix* the problem: *Take some time here to sense what is really going on for you...*

Conversely, if the client is experiencing the same old thing that you have been over together many times before, a question phrased in Solution Oriented language can be very useful for pattern interruption: *What will it look when it is right and no longer a problem?*

The ideal solution is to weave the language of both models together:

> *How will it look...feel...sound like when....?*

The words *look, feel,* and *sound like,* allow clients to process and respond in the way that is most natural to them: *visual, kinesthetic, or auditory.* (These three terms, visual, kinesthetic, and auditory, are referred to as the three "modalities" in the NLP lexicon.)

It is important to listen carefully for which of the three modalities clients use, in order to match your language to theirs. Most people access all three; however, there is usually an instinctive preference governing how people process information:

Visual:

> "I *see* what you mean"
> "What it *looks like* is..."
> "The way I *see it* is..."
> "My *image* is that..."

Kinesthetic:

"My *sense* of it is…"
"I *feel* that…"
"The way it *comes up* for me is…"
"I really *get* what you mean…"

Auditory:

"I *hear* what you're saying…"
"What it *sounds like* is..."
"I often *tell* my self…"
"A *voice* inside *says*…"

<u>Solution</u> language has a natural tendency to be visual:

THERAPIST: What do you *imagine*…it will look like…? (the Solution Picture)

CLIENT: The first thing I *see* is how much more confident I will look.

<u>Focusing</u> language has a natural tendency to be kinesthetic:

THERAPIST: What do you *sense*…about *how it will feel* when it's right?

CLIENT: I can just *feel* a kind of peace…right here in my stomach.

The use of auditory language can be reflected in either model (responding to the natural inclination of the client):

CLIENT: I *hear* what you're saying…but that's so hard for me to do.

THERAPIST: It *sounds* as if that poses a real dilemma for you.

Note: In Focusing we often combine modalities, for example: "Check and *see*… what's your *sense about…"*

If a client is primarily visual or auditory the therapist will find great value in adding a question that will produce a kinesthetic or *experiential response:*

THERAPIST: What's your *sense* of what will be different for you when you're *feeling* more creative and productive?

CLIENT: I will sit down and write for several hours each morning.

THERAPIST (Adds a question to produce an experiential response): Can you take a moment, now…to *sense…* what it *feels like* to be you… sitting at your desk…and writing each morning.

or:

THERAPIST: How do you imagine your husband will be when he sees you being more creative and writing again?

CLIENT: He will be so thrilled for me. I've been shutting him out because I've been in such a negative space.

THERAPIST (Adds a question to produce an experiential response): Can you *sense* what it will *feel like* to be welcoming your husband back into your space again…when you *feel* this renewed creativity?

Timing and modalities: In terms of *doing what comes naturally…*clients tend to respond differently on different days, in both pacing and how they use language. Sometimes they want to process and other times they just want to *talk* and *be heard.* The client is usually the best guide to determining what fits when, and what the best direction is to take. I have had clients actually ask for what they need at both ends of the Focusing and Solution spectrum: If I have posed a solution-type question at the *wrong moment,* I have had the client say:

You know…I'm not ready to find a solution yet. I just want to explore this more…take some time…to be with it.

At the other end, I have suggested an experiential *time-to-be-with* moment, and had the client say:

You know what, I'm sick to death of this. I don't really care what it's about anymore. I just need a solution!

The Solution Oriented therapist works from the outside in: as outer circumstances change (and/or the client's behavior) inner change will consequently occur.

The Focusing Oriented therapist works from the inside out: as the inner circumstances change (the client's relationship to him/her Self or to the issue) outer change will consequently occur.

Whether change ought to happen from the outside in, or vice versa, is a moot debate at best. *It doesn't matter!* Rather than promoting any particular theory of change, I like to use whichever model incorporates the natural inclination of the particular client(s); it usually turns out to be some combination of both (models). The success of either approach is informed by:

- ◊ The natural inclination of the client(s) and what they respond to best in therapy.
- ◊ The natural inclination of the therapist and what s/he feels most comfortable doing clinically.
- ◊ In the moment: what will work.

In the case of couples, where one partner expresses feelings easily, while the other is more cognitive and less emotive, it is advantageous for the therapist to be fluent in both languages. I refer to this fluency as being *bi-lingual* in order to be able to address people in a manner that speaks to their natural inclination (or "line of least resistance").

Tips

- ◊ Become fluent in both languages so that the bi-lingual process becomes seamless.
- ◊ Trust your own therapeutic style; i.e., how you naturally speak, and how you naturally connect with each of your clients in various circumstances.
- ◊ Be flexible and ready to adapt. I have had the experience during a session of adjusting my tone, speed, and the model I was using *mid-sentence,* if I sensed in the moment that the client was not responding to what I was doing.
- ◊ Trust your clients. They are your best guides.

Do whatever works best in the moment. Both approaches work; when integrated they work even better!

Affect: The Therapist/Client Relationship

As we continue exploring how to integrate and blend Experiential and Brief models of therapy, there is another point that needs to be recognized and acknowledged: The role that affect plays in a session is as relevant to the therapist as it is to the client.

I am not sure, if as clinicians, we 'choose' to incorporate the use affect into our work or if, by virtue of our own personalities and natural affinities, affect 'chooses us'! There are many varied and effective models of therapy and I suspect all of them probably work, at least some of the time. The more germane question is what draws us toward a particular model or set of models - or conversely, what steers us away from working with or in particular frameworks?

It would appear that the clinician's initial attraction toward any model (for our purposes Experiential or Brief Therapy) is probably influenced by the clinician's own natural comfort level with:

- ◊ Their client's expression of feelings during a session
- ◊ Their own expression of feelings during a session
- ◊ Self-disclosure, rather than presenting him/her self as "neutral"

There is no one 'right' way of practicing psychotherapy. For the practitioner, it is about finding ways of working that feel natural and in sync with his/her natural affinity and character. For the client, it is about how s/he feels in the presence of the therapist, i.e., feeling respected, listened to, and valued.

Both approaches accomplish this effortlessly, however it is important to note that there is a difference in style regarding the use of affect.

Experiential Therapy

In the experiential world, what comes first and foremost (and is the operative principle for any work that follows) is the establishing of the client/therapist relationship. The rapport between the therapist and client is considered to be so crucial to the success of therapy that it would probably be accurate to say that the whole field of Experiential Psychotherapy would be literally non-existent without the inclusion of affect (a natural inclination for therapists with experiential leanings).

As a result, the foundation of the therapeutic relationship is built on the premise that the therapist is authentic, genuine, and real. Rogers believed that for therapy "to be effective, it must be genuine" (Rogers, 1951). This authenticity includes: listening deeply and reflectively, with an attitude of what he termed as unconditional positive regard (Rogers, 1957); being with a client in an atmosphere of respect, caring, and empathic connection.

Through the therapist's valuing and respecting exactly how clients internally experienced their own realities, clients would find their true sense of self-acceptance leading to a right self-concept: how s/he would like to authentically be vs. an imposed false self-concept- how others would like him/her to be. Rogers believed that for genuine healing to occur, clients (and I might add, people in general) needed to feel a sense of affirmation and positive regard from others (Rogers, 1959).

Brief Therapy

In the Brief Therapy approach, joining is the operative word in establishing the initial connection with a client. It means finding common ground, finding common connections, finding areas of joint interest that allow the client to feel in sync and in rapport with the therapist.

From the Brief perspective, clients are coming to resolve specific issues, not to engage in profound relationships. The Brief therapist feels that the relationship will develop anyway through the process of respect and trust in the client's innate wisdom, and inherent competency in solving their own problems. "Joining" is simply a way to connect more quickly, or (as the saying goes) to "break the ice".

As already stated, the Brief therapist is helping the client focus on what is positive and right as related to the presenting problem, and encouraging the client to discover steps that are manageable and possible. Mutual respect, consideration and trust, are the equivalent to the empathic/affective relationship in the Experiential approaches.

In the end, the best and most effective clinicians are those who do whatever comes most naturally in relationship to their clients. What makes the therapy process meaningful for the client is authenticity on the part of the therapist.

Integrating Experiential and Brief Therapy

Art and life ought to be hurriedly remarried and brought to live together.

Hugh Walpole

Since the purpose of this book is to demonstrate the marriage of Experiential and Brief Therapy, perhaps the easiest way to learn it is by seeing what the integration looks like in practice. The following case examples are varied in content and approach, but the final resolution is always the blending and weaving of both models: Focusing and Solution Oriented Therapy.

Kyle was in his late 30's. He was, as he called it, "at the top of his game"; he was a success at every level. He had a Harvard Business degree, a wonderful family, was unusually attractive, and professionally had come very far, very fast. In a period of four years, he had worked his way up to Vice President of a large computer company, and was clearly slated for the top position when his boss stepped down.

The presenting problem: Kyle lost his job. The company had folded in the unexpected downward turn in technology stocks. A mega computer company had purchased Kyle's company, but Kyle was not in the new picture; his job was now "redundant". It was unthinkable and unimaginable, but it had happened.

Kyle was in shock. He felt devastated and depressed; he had assumed that his career path was stable. He had never been out of work and was faced with the harsh reality that finding another job at his level was more difficult than he had anticipated.

First Session:

KYLE: I'm so depressed…I can't eat, I can't sleep…I'm falling apart.

THERAPIST: There's a part of you that feels really down and depressed, right now… sort of like it's falling apart…

The therapist has already set up *the part* as separate from the whole in order to find out where Kyle can function better, separate from the depression. "Right now" assumes possible change.

KYLE: Yeah…it's a pretty huge part…

THERAPIST: So this depression part…*it's* taking up a huge amount of space, right now.

KYLE (picks up on the language immediately): Yeah…you know, that's right… it feels like it's everywhere…just looming everywhere… wherever I go, whatever I do…this depression…this mess…it's contaminating everything.

THERAPIST: It's looming everywhere…you can't seem to do anything when *it's* bigger than *you*…(points to I/it)

Kyle has had a small "Aha!". He has very slightly shifted his attention from depression as the problem, to *it* being bigger than *him* as the problem

THERAPIST: I'd like to ask if you can imagine something…you can close your eyes if you want to…to see it better…or not…is that OK? (He willingly closes his eyes.)…This issue…it's so big right now…and what is *wanted* is some space for you…a bit separate from *it*…so you can breathe a little…maybe begin to see all this in a different light…

The above suggestion is an *experiential version* of imaging the *Solution Picture.*

KYLE: It feels good just to be quiet for a bit…peaceful…there's so much noise in my head.

THERAPIST: Take a moment to enjoy...this *sense* that you are having of the peaceful place…away from the noise... (Kyle remains quiet for a while)

THERAPIST: See if you can get an image of...*All about this whole thing*...the issue...the part that feels so down and depressed...all of what you have to deal with in the days ahead...*the whole thing*...is there any image that just exactly fits *all of that?*

KYLE (gropes for awhile): ...I see Mt. Everest...it's so bloody huge...and I'm standing at the foot of it...I'm like an ant in relation to it...I feel so small... it's almost like I don't exist!

He's got a felt-sense: feeling like an ant at Mt. Everest.

THERAPIST: So this image of Mt. Everest...it's so huge...it makes you feel like an ant...like you don't exist...

KYLE: It's as if I've lost myself completely...

THERAPIST: It feels as if you've lost yourself completely...

KYLE: It's like I need to grow myself...I've become too small...

THERAPIST: It's something about being too small...you feel you need to grow yourself...

KYLE: Yes...that's it...I need to grow myself...(groping)...the image is changing now...ummm...I'm in a plane...I'm flying up high...over 30,000 feet and looking down at it...everything from a plane *looks smaller than it is!*

He has a bit of a felt-shift saying the words "smaller than it is".

THERAPIST: So the perspective changes...from 30,000 feet...Mt. Everest is smaller and you feel bigger...

KYLE: Ummm...perspective...yes, that's just the right word...I need to change the angle...look at this in a different way...

THERAPIST: So this is a really strong image...being up in that plane...

KYLE: Everything looks different from up here...I need to remember this...

THERAPIST: You want to remember this…to see…to sense…what you need to do…to keep seeing this *better view* of things…

Asking Kyle to consciously remember this *better view* of things is an *experiential* version of the action step.

KYLE: I need to stop and take some time to do what we are doing now…it's like…in trying to avoid the depression, I've been keeping myself almost too busy. Sort of…if I stop I might think about it…and if I think about it I'll lose control or something…maybe have a nervous breakdown, and be totally unable to cope.

THERAPIST (affirming him): So, *up to now,* keeping busy has actually been helpful, in a way…

KYLE: Yeah, but that's stupid isn't it…I mean…in trying not to think about it, it's just gotten bigger and bigger…

THERAPIST (reframes Critic): It's not stupid at all…in fact, it was pretty clever of you…like a coping strategy to protect yourself from feeling like you might get out of control…but now…something's changed…you have something that *will work better*…what's important now…is to take some *time for you*…to remember to view this from the new angle…

KYLE: I need to take time…I need to pilot that plane…I need height… take that plane as high up as I can…(laughs)…I guess I need to be bigger than Mt. Everest!

Comments:

This has been a good first session. He feels better than when he came in; he feels heard, and affirmed by the therapist, and he responds naturally to a Focusing Oriented approach:

◊ He can both image and sense easily.

◊ He has made a few significant shifts: experiencing the I/it connection, and finding a new distance from the issue; he now knows he needs to practice seeing himself as bigger than the issue.

While the first session set the tone for a positive start, his visualization efforts did not sustain him through the week. The therapist will continue with a Focusing orientation (because he responds well to it), however she will now add some Solution steps, as well.

Second Session:

KYLE: It worked for a while…but it didn't last…I'm very down again…and shrinking…

THERAPIST: Yes…this is a very big thing…not something that would disappear *all at once…*

"All at once" is meant as a segue into the Solution mode, i.e., if it is not *all at once,* perhaps he can look for "exceptions" or "small steps."

KYLE: I guess I wish it would disappear all at once…

THERAPIST: Yes, of course you do…but let's break down *all at once* into some smaller pieces…looking back over the week…was there *anytime at all* that you noticed you were *less* depressed…and *more* like yourself…?

First, the therapist is looking for the *exception* to the problem, focusing on *any time at all* that the problem wasn't happening. Second, by using the contrast of *less* and *more* the therapist points the client in the direction of a positive alternative.

KYLE: Oh…maybe…sometimes…

Kyle is slightly taken aback; he was totally unaware of any exceptions to the depression.

THERAPIST: Oh…really…sometimes…

The therapist is incorporating both models: reflecting experientially, and also "tracking" to pursue the exception.

KYLE: When I go to the park with my son…

Here is a spot that highlights very well the difference between the Focusing and Solution Oriented language. The reader might wish to take a moment here to sense the difference between the following:

Solution: "So you notice that you are less depressed and happier when you go to the park with your son."

Focusing: " *There's something there*...about going to the park with your son..."

This particular client adapts easily to experiential language. By saying "*there's something there*", the therapist is pointing to the felt-sense and giving him space to *grope* for what exactly that *something* is.

The therapist feels that the Solution Oriented question sounds too direct for the moment. The therapist will stay with *SOFT* language.

THERAPIST: There's *something there*…about going to the park with your son…

KYLE: Yeah…I like playing baseball with him…

THERAPIST (slowly): So there's *something you like*...about playing ball with him...

The therapist purposely slows down the process; she wants Kyle to both:

- ◊ Externally: Find the *exception* to the problem.
- ◊ Internally: Have him *sense/experience* what he's saying.

KYLE: This is a little embarrassing to say...but...my son...well, he just thinks I'm "the cat's meow"...(smiles)...So when we play ball together I feel important... competent...like a somebody...(pauses and looks directly at therapist for a moment) ...You know I'm pretty good at baseball...I used to be a star athlete (starts to noticeably change here as he goes into a reverie)... so I show him how to hold the bat...and catch...(He goes on with a lengthy description of teaching his son the game of baseball.)

Instead of reflecting his reverie, the therapist will take an *experiential leap*, reflecting *not his words*, but what she *senses* to be his *felt-meaning.*

THERAPIST: It sounds like the process of *teaching something*...that *you know so well*...makes you feel...*some way*...(Kyle gropes...)

KYLE: Useful! *(felt-shift)*...Yeah, that's it, I feel useful!

THERAPIST: You feel useful...(he nods)...and that is a wonderful feeling...*right here*...can you take a moment to just have it for yourself...this useful feeling that *makes you feel so good.*

Kyle takes an *experiential moment* before the therapist continues with a Solution question.

THERAPIST: Maybe notice...where else in your life...you have this good feeling... like...*useful?*

KYLE: Well...I'm teaching my daughter how to use the computer...(then suddenly adds)...and since I've been home more...I'm getting pretty inventive in the kitchen!

Comments:

Kyle's energy has shifted from feeling useless to useful, from depressed to hopeful.

The Focusing approach helped him to connect meaningfully with his feelings: what was painful, as well as good.

The Solution approach helped to keep Kyle's attention on what was good and possible.

The most frustrating part of this type of case is that there is no quick fix, no direct solution to the problem of finding a job. What is possible is helping him to stay in the best frame of mind he can maintain until he does find work - which he eventually did!

CASE: VICKY

Vicky, an English teacher, was in her early 50's, happily married for 26 years with three grown children, two sons and a daughter. Her concerns were about her mother and her 55-year-old brother.

Vicky's issues with her mother were complicated. Her mother had been difficult at the best of times: demanding, controlling, and unreasonable. According to Vicky, these qualities were exacerbated after the death of Vicky's father. Sarah (her Mom) always favored her son Ted, and took every opportunity to let Vicky know that whatever she did was "never good enough". Vicky had spent most of her life trying to get her mother's approval, which she felt she never received.

Vicky's brother, Ted, had moved to London, England, ten years ago, for a job. The move left Vicky with all the responsibility for her mother, which was considerable. She'd seen her mother through a long drawn-out illness, which eventually required having to sell Sarah's home, and move her to full-time care in a nursing home.

Vicky had come into therapy to try to reconcile her feelings about her dying mother, and her building resentment toward her brother. As it came to pass, her mother died between the first and second session. Between the third and fourth session, Vicky had learned that Sarah's will had not been divided equally; her brother received a larger portion of the estate. Vicky was outraged and hurt, especially since she had shouldered the bulk of the responsibility for her mother for so many years. She also felt that her brother's behavior had been "slippery" around the issue of the will; he had known for some time that he was getting more money, and should have told her.

After the funeral, Ted and his wife decided to leave London and move back home; they wanted to be closer to Vicky and her husband, as well as their niece and nephews, especially since they had no children of their own. Vicky had already been working in therapy on her relationship with her mother and her brother. She was emotional and reactive by nature, and acknowledged often that she "speaks before she thinks".

While using experiential listening to make sure that Vicky felt heard, the therapist leaned toward a Solution Oriented approach in order to lower the intensity on her affective state.

Fifth Session:

VICKY: I want to work on my relationship with my brother today. I want a relationship with him…but I'm fearful…it doesn't feel safe…I'm afraid to open up...I'm afraid of losing it…of getting too emotional…

THERAPIST: So there's a lot *there*. Part of you wants to have a relationship with your brother and another part feels afraid to do that…like you might lose it, and be too emotional…

VICKY: If I lose it…I'm so afraid of what I might say to him…I'm so resentful about the money…about so many things…

This is a *crossroads* where the therapist needs to make a judgment call about which model to use. If the therapist chooses a Focusing approach a possible question might be:

> *Of the two parts, the part that wants to connect with him and the part that doesn't…can you sense which one has the most energy right now…*

If Vicky says that it is the *fear part…the one that's afraid of losing it*, the therapist might suggest that she make room for the part that is carrying the fear, allowing an opening for Vicky to work with: *What is so fearful?* and *What does it need?*

In this case, the therapist chooses to take a Solution approach. She wants to help Vicky see the bigger picture. Vicky is already highly emotional; she and the therapist have spent a fair amount of time paying attention to Vicky's feelings. The therapist chooses a systemic approach. She wants to understand Vicky's relationship with the larger family unit. She also wants to help Vicky reframe the issue in the context of the family situation.

THERAPIST: I can't help wondering…if your whole family was here with us now… what do you imagine each of them would have to say about all of this?

VICKY: Let's see…my husband, Martin, would like to see Ted and I reconcile our differences…but Martin is very low key…he'd never push it. Our youngest son, Brian, and our daughter Millie, would be like my husband…they'd like to see this resolved for the sake of the whole family…but they know what I've been through and they'd never push…

THERAPIST: OK…so far, your husband and two of your kids are very supportive of you…they'd like to see a reconciliation…but they would never push you to do anything you didn't want to do.

VICKY: Yes. It's David, my eldest, that's the problem. He's very close with his Uncle Ted…he was also the closest to my mother…he has very definite ideas about family and closeness, and spending the holidays together…

THERAPIST: So David has some very definite ideas about how he wants this family to be…together.

VICKY: Yes. He's sort of blaming me…that we're not having Ted and Kathy (Ted's wife) over all the time… like it's because of me - and only me. He never blames Ted for anything…but it's so hard for me…The holidays were so tense this year…I could hardly look Ted in the eye throughout the whole meal.

THERAPIST: Let me ask you something…can you take a minute to imagine…that is…see what your vision is…about what it would look like if it was right with Ted?

> The therapist has asked the question in a Focusing-process-style, but has avoided the use of the words "feel" or "sense". Vicky is already overly reactive. Instead, keeping in line with the idea of "seeing the bigger picture", the therapist purposely chooses words like "imagine", "vision" and "look like".

VICKY: We'd be friends again…we used to be quite close as children.

THERAPIST (pins it down): Maybe you could help me here…I'm not sure what you mean by "friends". What do you imagine will be happening when you are friends, again?

The therapist's own felt-sense is one of warning: she suspects that Vicky's and Ted's meaning of the word "friends" may not be the same. The therapist will pursue this in a Solution Oriented way.

VICKY: If we were friends again…well, these are some of the things I imagine… We'd talk on the phone…maybe every other day…We'd share deeply about our lives and our feelings…like we used to as kids…we were so much closer as kids. There would be trust and compassion between us…and we'd want to see each other a lot. He and Kathy would probably come over for dinner on Friday nights...and maybe we'd occasionally take trips together…we'd really be like *best friends*.

The therapist was right in feeling a sense of caution, and is now certain that Vicky's and her brother's vision/version of "friendship" are not in sync. The therapist will proceed "weaving" their points of view in a circular pattern.

THERAPIST: Let's just imagine that your brother was here with us right now. He's sitting right there on the couch, next to you…and I ask him, *Ted, what does it mean to you to be friends again with your sister?*

VICKY: He'd say, "Maybe we'd talk on the phone once a week or so… and have family dinners once or twice a month. I certainly don't want to be as emotionally close as my sister demands…I guess I'd like to be…pleasant friends."

As soon as Vicky hears herself say the words "pleasant friends" she loses her brother's voice, and burst into an angry tirade. Also, she did not hear herself use the word "demands", but the therapist thought that was a very *telling* word.

VICKY: I don't want to keep sweeping it under the rug! Oh! He makes me so mad…he just won't deal with *anything!!*

THERAPIST (tentatively): I'm not sure if you're meaning about this issue…with your mother…or all the time…

VICKY: All the time…he's always been like that…he's so damn super?cial… he likes family gatherings as long as they're *pleasant* (she exaggerates the word)...he likes anything as long as it's pleasant…but sharing his feelings? Going deeply into anything?…He's incapable…he can't share himself in any meaningful way…

THERAPIST: So really, there's *something* that you *want*...this deep sharing...that he's *not able*...or *not wanting*...to do...never has...

VICKY (bursts into tears, and has a *felt-shift* at the same time): I see it...I always want the impossible!...It's not just with my brother...I do this in the family all the time...I decide how things should be, and then of course they are never that way...and then I feel disappointed...or ripped off...(gets very quiet here)...I have to think about this.

Therapist and Vicky are both quiet for some time. The therapist then uses the *SOFT* approach: asking a Solution question in a Focusing way.

THERAPIST (gently): Vicky, maybe take a minute here to see...if your brother could tell you now...what you could do...that would be helpful to him in this relationship...what do you imagine he would say?

VICKY: He'd say that he'd like me to listen better to what he has to say...to take the time to consider what he says before reacting...he'd say I'm overly emotional.

THERAPIST: So he'd say that he wants you to listen better...to consider what he's saying in a less emotional way...

VICKY: That's exactly what he would say...

THERAPIST: And when you are doing that... *listening better*...and reacting less... what do you suppose will be different then?

VICKY (another explosion of tears and another *shift*): I'd act like a grown-up instead of a child!...I'm always trying to get reassurance and approval. I did that with my mom for my whole life...I do it with *everybody!*...and I'm doing it with my brother now...(more tears)

Another therapeutic *judgment call:* If the therapist had been using the Focusing Oriented approach, she might have gone in any number of directions here: working with the inner-child part; having the grown-up part and child-part dialogue; or having Vicky stay with the pain, and explore her feelings.

The therapist may do this some time in the future, however at this juncture, the therapist feels that Vicky needs to lower the volume on her emotional life. The therapist now attempts to build a Solution Picture with Vicky in order to give her a wider perspective. (In Focusing this is called seeing "the whole of it.")

THERAPIST: Can you *imagine a time in the future*, when it is *all OK*...when the *need is gone* to get approval and reassurance…when you are *being, acting, and feeling* the way *you know you want to.* Check and see…what *will be happening* then, that isn't happening now?

VICKY: (sighs, and makes a list with her eyes closed): I will…

◊ be more self-confident be more creative…I love to make crafts

◊ stop procrastinating…I'm using about half of my potential

◊ be more motivated to do things that I want to do for me

◊ take more risks…not be so fearful of failing, or worried about not being good enough

◊ be thinking more creatively…expressing myself more openly with friends and family

THERAPIST: That's a wonderful long list of possibilities…let's make a scale and see where you are with this, right now. On a scale of one to ten…if ten was you being your best, creative, most productive self, and one was everything you don't want…where would you say you'd realistically like to be?

VICKY: An eight or a nine…I have so much going for me…and a loving family… I really could do anything…if I'd just put my mind to it.

What I don't want 1______________**8**_**9**_10 Creative, best self

THERAPIST (checking): So your *sense* is that an eight or nine would be very realistic…(Vicky nods)

THERAPIST: Can you check and see where you are on the scale right now?

VICKY: I guess somewhere around a four.

1______**4**_____________10

THERAPIST: What do you imagine you'll need to do… between now, and the next time we meet, that would put you at a solid four and a half …maybe even a five?

VICKY: I need to stop blaming my mother and my brother, and grow up!

The *action step* has to be *doable*; she can *not* do "growing up". Clients often have a *concept* of what will make it better; it is the therapist's job to pin it down into *concrete* action steps that can actually be accomplished.

THERAPIST: So when you are not blaming your mother and your brother…what do you suppose you'll be doing instead?

VICKY: Ummm…I'll pay more attention to myself and my own needs…maybe I'll go out and buy some art supplies, and make something I've been wanting to make.

THERAPIST: So you are saying that paying more attention to your own wants and needs…and maybe buying some art supplies and making something…will bring you from a four to a four and a half on the scale…

VICKY: Yes. I've been wanting to paint a small mural on the wall of the upstairs hallway…I've been putting it off forever…I'd really like to do it.

THERAPIST: OK…it sounds like you have a plan and you are wanting to get started. When do you imagine you'll begin?

VICKY: I'm going to stop at the store as soon as I leave here…it's right on my way home, and I know exactly what I need!

Comments:

The *SOFT* approach has worked very well here. While the therapist remained empathic and connected, she felt it was essential to use a Solution approach to help Vicky:

- ◊ think things through more carefully
- ◊ become less emotional and reactive
- ◊ learn how to take concrete action steps
- ◊ shift her energy away from her mother and brother (with whom she had become somewhat obsessed)
- ◊ become more focused on what she needed to do for herself

Vicky continued to concentrate more on her own creative endeavors: painting, sculpting, and making stained glass. As she became less fixated on her brother, and what he was doing and feeling, he began to feel more comfortable in her company, more of the time. Her most challenging task was learning to accept that he was "allowed" to share his feelings - or *not*. As she became less intrusive, he quite naturally became more open to her.

Vicky eventually conceded that she knew and understood why her brother had received a larger portion of the will. Vicky and her husband were financially solvent; money was not an issue for them, and probably never would be. Their children were already successful professionals, and financially independent; it was unlikely that they would be a financial drain on their parents.

Ted on the other hand, had never been financially successful. His mother's hope was that he would move back from Europe to be closer with the family, and use the extra money to buy his first house. Vicky eventually accepted the reasoning behind her mother's actions.

CASE: MIKE

Mike is forty-seven years old. He started working in junior high school, and has been hard working ever since. His wife, to whom he was devoted, died of cancer about two years prior to his coming into therapy. His two adult sons live in different parts of the country. Mike currently lives alone.

He was the head foreman in a machine factory. While helping a new employee learn how operate a particular machine, a terrible accident occurred: the machine blew up, fell on him, and for a time he was trapped under the machine.

His femur (thigh bone) was severed, causing bone death. Subsequently, after several surgeries, Mike's hip had to be replaced. There was also some soft tissue damage and a broken ankle.

He had been with a previous therapist for about three months. The therapist's diagnosis was Post Traumatic Stress Disorder. Mike also suffered from nightmares, flashbacks, bouts of uncontrollable sweating, then chills; he was exhausted.

He was not the type of individual who would ever seek out or even consider therapy on his own, even after the loss of his wife. He was in therapy on "doctor's orders" and wasn't sure what to expect from the therapy process. He was very clear with the new therapist that he didn't feel he had made any progress in his first round of therapy and was, he admitted, "totally fed up."

The therapist was faced with an interesting dilemma in this case. On one hand, Mike was most definitely a pragmatist, not a "therapy-type", which he had made clear from the start. On the other hand, the therapist felt that he needed to be heard experientially - in spite of the fact that this was not Mike's style at all. (Notice the progression from Mike's responses at the beginning of the session, to his reflection about the usefulness of the session, at the very end.)

The new therapist had known some of the story before Mike came into therapy, but sensing that he very much needed to tell his story, she invited him to recount freshly what had happened. He concluded with...

MIKE: So I was thinking, *God, I'm going to die...I'm really going to die.*

THERAPIST: My God! You are such a brave man…to go through such a terrible ordeal…

The orientation in Focusing is to establish a relationship: empathy, caring, connectedness, and *being real*. The therapist is truly astounded by this story, and makes no attempt to be "neutral".

MIKE: I was terrified…All I can see is that big machine…day and night…I just see that machine…

THERAPIST: Yes, I can imagine…that machine represents so many things…

MIKE: Yeah, everything…my job, my health, my state of mind… everything... but all I can think about is that machine…Oh, it was big…that's all I can see is that big god damned machine…

At this juncture the therapist has no idea of how to proceed, or what direction to take. She's trying to get "a feel" for him, and what he wants, and finally asks him directly.

THERAPIST: Mike, I'd really like to be helpful to you. This is such a huge thing… that you've experienced…and I need your help in understanding what you are *wanting* now…Is it about not wanting to see the machine anymore? Or is it wanting to feel some other way…?

MIKE: Yeah, I want it to not have happened. I want to go back to the way things were, and I want to go back to my job…I've been there twenty-seven years, and I don't want to give that up…but I have to…

THERAPIST: Of course you want it to be the way it was…This is such a difficult situation…a very huge loss…of many things…

The therapist feels that it is inappropriate to bypass the affective component in this case, or to go searching for solutions too quickly. She chooses to move into a Focusing Oriented process.

THERAPIST: Mike, I want to say a few things to you: This thing that happened to you…this accident…it never should have happened…*never*…you didn't deserve this…and it wasn't your fault. It happened, yes, and it shouldn't have…(Mike is very quiet, just taking in the therapist's words.)…I know this is going to sound a bit odd…what I am going to say to you now…but there's a *part* of you that has to carry around this terrible burden…and this *part*…it just feels so awful…it seems so unjust and unfair… this part feels as if he's carrying around the weight of the world right now…Mike, do you understand what I'm meaning if I say: Can you just make some room in there for the part of you that has to carry this weight, and maybe be a little…patient and kind with him…

MIKE: I have a hard time with patience, but every day…yeah…that's what I'm doing every day.

THERAPIST: I guess when I say *patient and kind*…it would be as if you had a kid who had an accident…and maybe he lost a leg…imagine that for a moment… a wonderful child that you love very much comes to you, crying. He says that it's really not fair, because everyone else…all his friends...are playing baseball...and he can't play. And you're feeling frustrated. You love him, you want to help him, it shouldn't have happened…AND…*it did happen*…and you want to find a way to show him…how he's OK…even with one leg…

The therapist wants to help Mike make a separation between the part that is devastated and his higher functioning Self. She senses that her suggestion to *make room for the part* that has to carry around the issue is not enough. She then frames the part as *a child* that he loves, hoping that such a powerful image will help him to make that separation.

MIKE: I don't want to, but I can.

THERAPIST: This is very important...what you're saying: "I don't want to, but *I can.*"

MIKE: I don't have a choice.

THERAPIST: It's true...that it doesn't seem like there's much choice...but there is *a part there*...that has some acceptance in it...it's the part that says, *I can.*

This is such a small, but crucial, first step. The therapist is attempting to plant the seeds for a future time when Mike will be able to affirm that there is a part of him that *can* handle this situation.

THERAPIST: I'd like to ask you to do something here - is that OK?

MIKE: Sure, why not...I've got nothing to lose...

THERAPIST: Good. Can you take a minute here to *sense* something: There's one part of you that says, *I can,* and another part that says, *it never should have happened.* Which of those two feels the strongest to you, right now?

MIKE: It's in the part that says, *this should never have happened.*

When dealing with *parts* always ask the client which of them is the strongest, or has the most energy, in the moment. This is something the therapist *cannot know* without asking.

THERAPIST: Again...this may sound a bit odd, but...would it be OK if we tried to talk to it...the part...?

MIKE: Sure. (He has no idea what is going on, but is totally engaged.)

THERAPIST: OK...so we want to pretend that this part...the one that says, *it never should have happened*... is like another person...like a *real person*...and you and I are going to have a conversation with him...

The therapist includes herself in the conversation by saying "we". Having an inner dialogue is so foreign to him that if he feels like he is alone, talking to himself, he may feel awkward, or worse, downright crazy!

THERAPIST: So we want to start by saying...acknowledging...that this is the most terrible, devastating and unfair thing in the whole world...and it never should have happened.

MIKE: You're right about that...it shouldn't have happened...

THERAPIST: No…it shouldn't have…but it did…and now…we want to help him feel better at every level…so many levels…there is the physical, and all the pain that goes with the accident…there is the emotional, the shock and the fear…and there's the mental...the worry…the nightmares…

MIKE: It's too big…there's too much…it's my whole life…

THERAPIST: Yes…well put, that's exactly the point…it *is* too big…so we can only work on a little piece at a time. We are just looking for one small step…*just one thing*…that would help him feel a little bit better, right now…what's your sense…if that part could speak…of what he'd say he needs…

MIKE: He would say he needs to make sure he's got a job. He'd say he's really worried about that...(shifts to "I")…I don't want to hang around on disability for the rest my life…

THERAPIST: So that's a real concern…having a job…would you mind my asking… Is that request in the realm of possibility?

The therapist has just gone through a long experiential suggestion, imaging that he will say something like: he needs to be more patient or kind. Instead his *one small thing* is not so small - he wants a job. The therapist has no idea whether his answer is simply "wishful thinking", or within the realm of possibility, so she asks him.

MIKE: Yeah…it is…I've got contacts…and when I feel ready…like OK in the head…it's a real possibility.

THERAPIST: So that's very real…that you can work again…

MIKE: Yeah…but being ready…I don't know…

THERAPIST: It's important to know that this isn't about looking for a job today…we just want to take the tiny step of exploring a world in which you can handle this…the world of, *Yes, I can.*

MIKE (smiles for the first time): Yeah, I like that.

Comments:

There are a number of things to notice about what the therapist did.

First, although this session was primarily experiential, the therapist took a very active role in the session - more than is usual in the Focusing Oriented approach. She knew that he was not impressed with his first round of therapy, and tried to engage him by "doing something different" (a Solution expression).

Second, the therapist sensed that Mike needed to be heard at a deep level that acknowledged the severity of his trauma. Her hope was that through the process of listening, she would find something positive to latch on to (the proverbial "needle in the haystack").

After the session was over, the therapist did something unusual. She "interviewed" Mike to get his impressions of the session. Here are some excerpts from that interview:

THERAPIST: It would help me to know if what we did felt useful to you?

MIKE: I can see how…there were these thoughts going through my mind…I wanted to make sure that you knew…this isn't in my head, it really did land on me - it really did blow apart…and it's affected my whole life…

THERAPIST: And did you feel that I really got it…that you knew I didn't think it was just in your head?

MIKE: Yeah, it was when you said, *this never should have happened.* It made a world of difference.

THERAPIST: So that was important to you. Can you say why?… because that's really important for me to understand.

MIKE: It made a world of difference, because one of the things I wanted through all of this…was someone to just understand…even though I've had a lot of support…I've felt very alone in this, like…how many people could understand what it's like to have this machine blow up in your face…this was the most horrendous, negative experience that could have happened to me… It was something like…this could happen to someone else, but not to me… sort of like…it's just not acceptable…and when you said that, *it never should have happened,* and that *it wasn't right*…to hear that said out loud…it's hard to explain…it made me feel like I wasn't crazy…or making too much of it…I'm a pretty tough guy.

THERAPIST: I just want you to know that I really meant what I said. It shouldn't have happened…and you are one of the bravest people I have ever met...I don't know…if something like that happened to me…if I could handle it as well as you have…I mean that…

MIKE: I really appreciate your saying that…you know, there's something else… it's about the way that you listen…you know when I said, *I don't want to, but I can.* That wasn't a big deal when I said it…I just said it in passing…but you kind of made a big deal of it…I mean that in a good way…and I feel now…just a little bit more hope…like…maybe I really can!

In subsequent sessions, the therapist built upon the "I can". During the first session the issue was huge and the "I can" was miniscule. Over time the therapist worked with Mike to shrink the huge part (the accident), help him feel ready to work in a new job (about which he had reservations and fears), and build up *what is possible.*

CASE: MELISSA

Melissa is an exceptionally beautiful, single, 35 year old buyer for an international clothing chain. Her greatest desire is to be married with children. She has a knack for finding men who are needy or "OK except for *just one thing"* (usually major). She has had an ongoing stream of dysfunctional relationships - "I keep picking losers" is how she presented it to the therapist.

Melissa was adopted at birth. Her mother had a hysterectomy after the birth of her son who was three years older than Melissa. Tragedy struck the family when Melissa was ten years old: her adoptive father, with whom she was very close, died suddenly of heart failure. Although Melissa understood that she was wanted and loved, she had trouble coming to terms with being "given up" for adoption. That, coupled with the unexpected loss of her father, made her struggle with feelings of abandonment an ongoing theme throughout her life.

Her mother, who felt sometimes overwhelmed as a single parent to two children, was caring but also over-functioning and, according to Melissa, overly critical of her. While Melissa's mother genuinely loved both her children, after her husband died she began to bond more with her son who became the "man of the house". According to Melissa her brother, in her mother's eyes, "could do no wrong". Concurrently, in her mother's eyes, Melissa felt she "could do no right". She learned how to lie, manipulate, and get out of jams for which she felt she would be blamed. She had an edge of defensiveness: *I didn't do it,* or *it's not my fault* which colored everything she did on a personal level.

Somehow she managed to compartmentalize the personal and professional aspects of her life. Melissa learned to be responsible in certain specific areas. She was impeccable at work where she was continually given more responsibility and promotions. She bought her own home and took great care in fixing it up, especially the garden, which was her great joy and accomplishment. She was also responsible, for the most part, with money and savings.

However, she had a compulsion to be irresponsible and reckless. She would go on drinking binges during which she would take outrageous and dangerous risks: driving home almost senselessly drunk, picking up strange men and taking them to hotels, passing out with no memory of what she had done, or what had happened to her.

She did not view herself as an alcoholic. She was able to go through long periods of either drinking normally, or not drinking at all. She viewed her behavior as a "wanting to kill" a part of her that she "hated", and said that when the urge to be destructive came, it was sometimes "overwhelming".

The Focusing and Solution Oriented models would each have very different interpretations and approaches for managing this case.

The Solution Oriented therapist might reframe Melissa's "compulsion" as a "bad habit", and would look for ways to find alternative, and more useful "behaviors". The therapist would externalize the behavior, making "it" the problem instead of Melissa: (This is similar to the "I/it" relationship in Focusing) sometimes the *behavior* is *bigger* than her; sometimes *she* is bigger than the behavior.

The Focusing Oriented therapist might view the situation this way: Melissa's Critic was out of control, and had entirely over-shadowed her ability to function as the core Self or "adult". The Critic, who was now in charge, was raising the child-part in a destructive and abusive fashion. The therapist would need to help Melissa find and access her adult-Self.

From the outset, Melissa's therapist has integrated both models in their sessions. Melissa is very familiar and comfortable with experiential work and understands the concept of "parts"; she also responds well to the Solution Oriented approach, especially in regard to setting goals and taking concrete steps.

The therapist has worked with Melissa for well over a year. They have a strong connection; and from the clinician's point of view Melissa is an ideal client: open, searching, wanting change, and willing to deeply explore the issues that prevent her from reaching her various goals. Melissa also has a quick and easy sense of humor, and the sessions are often punctuated with amusing moments.

MELISSA: I did something really bad…it's so bad…I feel embarrassed to tell you…

To the therapist's ear this sounds like a child who has just been beaten up by a Critic. (Melissa often refers to the child-part as "the younger one".)

THERAPIST: I think perhaps there is a Critic here…maybe we should start by imagining the *younger one* is wanting to tell you something…something that *she* did, that *she* regretted…

MELISSA: Oh…she regrets it alright…she really screwed up this time…

THERAPIST: Yes, I know *she's* feeling awful, right now, but let's try to get our characters straight, alright...so that it is *you* who is talking to me, and not a Critic...if *you* were listening to that *younger part*…and being caring…and she said she had something she wanted to tell you…but it wasn't good… what would you want say to her?

MELISSA (pauses to sort it out): OK…I think I'm getting to a righter place…I'd tell her that she could tell me anything...and that I'd listen to her…and that she shouldn't be afraid…

THERAPIST: Good…so can you ask *her* to tell *you*…us…the story now…?

MELISSA: Yeah, OK…I…(exaggerates)…I mean *she*…really did something awful…*she* was so mean to a good friend…(pauses) I need to tell you this as *I*...

THERAPIST: OK…that's fine.

Because Melissa is about to tell a story that a child would not be telling, she wants to tell it as "I". This happens frequently when working with parts. It is perfectly acceptable to have the client tell the story in the first person. Later, the therapist can ask *how the part* (that did the negative behavior) *feels about all that.*

MELISSA: This friend told me that she was interested in this man, a guy she really liked…so the three of us - my friend, the guy she liked, and me - were all out for drinks…I got drunk and started to flirt with him mercilessly…and did some really stupid things…that I can't bear to say…

THERAPIST: This is a tough one…it's really hard to bear it when you do something you just totally regret…it feels so awful…so if it's OK with you I'd like to say something to the child…

The therapist speaks directly to the child for two reasons. First, to keep the space safe: the therapist knows that the Critic is on the brink of an attack. Second, the therapist often models the adult-part for Melissa, who is still working on developing a more functional adult-self, which Melissa often refers to as "growing her adult".

MELISSA: That sounds really good…because I sure as hell don't know what to say to her…

THERAPIST (talking to the "younger one"): Sometimes...we do things that we really feel awful about afterwards...and that's kind of normal....doing things we wish we hadn't done. But what I want to say to you now is…there are *no mistakes*…only *learning* and *growing*. It's not about *right and wrong*…it's about…*What can I learn from this that will help me next time?* Does that make any sense?"

MELISSA: I do know this…but I keep forgetting it…

THERAPIST: Yes, I know…sometimes learning something new…changing patterns…takes a while…Can we try again…?

MELISSA: Yes…boy, I'd sure love to get this right…

THERAPIST: OK, can you tell that part of you that acts out…that you understand sometimes she does inappropriate things…and that you know how frightened she gets about doing these things…

Melissa takes some quiet time to internalize the words.

THERAPIST: Let her know that you really would like to help her…to work together with her so you can both feel better…and then gently ask her… What it is that makes her act that way…?

MELISSA: She says that it's the only way she can get my attention. She says that I ignore her and desert her.

THERAPIST (reflects back): She's feeling ignored and deserted. She wants your attention…and doesn't know how she can get it…

MELISSA: She says that no matter how crazy she acts…no matter how many tantrums she has…she can't get my attention…She says if she tried to kill herself, she doesn't think I would notice…she feels that abandoned and alone…

THERAPIST: Can you ask her what would happen…if somehow, you could agree to make a commitment to her…to pay attention to her…

MELISSA (interrupts): She doesn't buy it. She says I've made commitments to her before and I'm totally unreliable…She feels ripped off, and doesn't trust me at all...SHE doesn't want to have a relationship with ME!

THERAPIST: Mmmm…that is a predicament…so I need to ask YOU here…Did you ever get really angry with your own mom...and maybe say something awful to her…something you regretted afterward?

MELISSA (laughs): All the time! I was an awful kid, you know, and my mom had a rough time…single mother to me and my brother, who was of course (exaggerates) "a model child"…ughhh…I really was a monster…

THERAPIST: Did your Mom forgive you?

MELISSA: Always, although I don't know why…

THERAPIST: Why do you think…?

MELISSA: I guess she really loved me…no…I don't guess, I know…she really did love me…she does love me…even though she can be so critical sometimes… ughhh…she drives me crazy…But I know that she just wants my life to work out…(gets weepy here)...That's the same for me and the inner-part, too, isn't it? That's what you're trying to get me to see…that I can't give up on her…?

THERAPIST: What do you think?

MELISSA: Yeah…but what if *she* doesn't want to have anything to do with *me*?

THERAPIST: What did your mom do when you didn't want to have anything to do with her?

MELISSA: She hung in there...she waited…Sometimes she came into my room at bedtime for "a little chat"…OK, what do I have to do…?

THERAPIST: Shall we try to go back to a process-place?

MELISSA (closes her eyes): Yeah, why not…

When an experiential process has been interrupted, it is important to ask the client to *check freshly*, to see where they are in the moment. One reason is that the therapist cannot possibly know without asking; another reason is that, from an experiential perspective, the client won't necessarily pick up where they left off.

THERAPIST: I'm not sure where exactly you want to start…maybe check freshly, and see where you are, right now…

MELISSA: I think I need to apologize to her…

THERAPIST: OK then…why don't you just sit for a minute, and let the words form…what you really want to say to her, right now…

MELISSA: I want to tell her not to give up on me …(gets weepy again)…I want to tell her that I'm a shitty adult…but I'm working on it…I want to tell her that I'm not a model parent, but I'm all she has...and she's all I have…so somehow we have to do this together…sort of help each other out…

THERAPIST: Does she have anything to say to that…?

MELISSA: She says she's not a wimp…she says she can deal with almost anything…but she doesn't want to do it alone…she says I'm not a half bad adult (laughs), but she needs me to pay attention to her…listen to her…not quit on her…

THERAPIST: Can you ask her…when you are really paying more regular attention to her…when you are listening to her, and being there for her…consistently… what kind of a difference will that make to her?

Although still in a process-mode, the therapist has switched to Solution Oriented language; she uses "when" and "will", assuming change. Focusing Oriented language would purposefully be more tentative: "*if* you were paying more attention..."

MELISSA: She says she will feel like she is worth something…she says she often feels worthless…

THERAPIST: She says she will feel worth something…she'll feel…of *value*…?… to herself and to you.

The therapist stays with positive language by avoiding the word "worthless" and instead, suggests tentatively, "of *value...?*" If Melissa doesn't "buy it" she'll go back to the word "worthless". If she does "buy it" they will continue on a positive track. In this case, she does.

MELISSA: I like that word "value"…I don't use it very much. I think that's why I pick such crappy men...a part of me feels like I don't deserve any better…

THERAPIST (pursuing): So when she's feeling cared about and valued by you… what kind of difference will that make to her?

MELISSA: She says she'll behave herself…(she's surprised by her own answer)

THERAPIST: Really…?

MELISSA: She says she won't need to *act out* to get my attention, because if I keep my promise she'll already have my attention.

THERAPIST: Mmmm...So when she's behaving and acting in a better way...how will that affect your life...?

MELISSA: I'll trust myself...I'll really trust myself...I've never ever trusted myself...I *really believe* I'd trust myself...

THERAPIST: You'd really trust yourself...and that sounds new (suggests a quick experiential moment)...maybe just take a minute here to be with...*I really believe I'll trust myself...*(After a minute the therapist continues with Solution language)...So when you are really trusting yourself...knowing you can count on yourself to do the right thing...what do you suppose you'll be doing that you're not doing now?

MELISSA: I won't be afraid to take ownership...

This is one of those lines that either kinesthetically means something, or just sounds right cognitively, but the body hasn't got it yet. The therapist makes sure that Melissa takes the time to internalize what she's saying.

THERAPIST: See what that actually *means* to you: *I won't be afraid to take ownership*...imagine what that will be like...

MELISSA: I'll be responsible...I'll act responsibly...and I'll stop putting *her* in positions where she really could get killed...God!...do you realize some of the things that I've done...?

She's just on the verge of another Critic attack; the therapist steps in immediately.

THERAPIST (pursuing): You'll be responsible, you'll act responsibly, and you'll protect her at all cost...

MELISSA (bolts out of the process): The *compulsion* to abdicate responsibility will be gone!

THERAPIST (pursues more): See what *that means* to you, when you say, *The compulsion to abdicate responsibility will be gone.*

MELISSA: Well for one thing, I'll enjoy a glass of wine like a normal person… I'll feel like a normal person…Lord! Maybe I can actually *be* a normal person!!

THERAPIST: It's about being normal…and that's always been an odd word for you…(The therapist already knows this from other conversations.)

MELISSA: It sure has…I always think I'm a secret nutcase…and nobody knows… The word "normal" has never felt like anything I'm entitled to.

THERAPIST: So "normal" has a new sound to you right now. Can we say that you are embarking on a study of "new normal"…that is…what "normal" means to you?

MELISSA: Oh, I love that…"new normal"…very neat!

THERAPIST: So may I give you a little homework here?

MELISSA: Absolutely!…even *she* says she won't mind doing homework - ha ha!

THERAPIST: OK…so, will you do some research on the word "normal"? I don't mean book research. Speak to people: friends, colleagues, your mother, your brother - anyone who seems to know something about what's normal for them.

Let me be more specific: If you want to know how much drinking is "normal", ask people you respect, how much they actually drink, especially on week-nights…If you want to know what's "normal" in terms of how many men your single women friends sleep with - ask the ones you feel date responsibly…If you want to know what "normal" people do to fight self-destructive urges - find people who've done that, and ask them...and write it down! (She likes to write.) This is about once and for all finding a "new normal" that really fits for you…that your *body buys*.

MELISSA: You give very good homework! So maybe I'll be an "A student"… Yeah, yeah, I know… (mimics therapist) "Small manageable steps". OK I'll be a "B student" for our next session…ha ha!

Comments:

Melissa is a highly complicated individual. She works consistently with the therapist on integrating the disparate parts of herself, and developing a competent "adult-self" that can manage a sometimes out-of-control "child-part".

As the "younger one", she is prone to extremely dysfunctional behavior: depression, rage, and self-destructive urges. Her "high-maintenance Critic", as she calls it, is mean, cynical, and makes every effort to sabotage her natural, joyful and high-spirited self. The Critic frames its actions as "protection", so that she *won't do something stupid - again.*

As the work continues, Melissa is gradually building a strong and more solid core Self that is increasingly able to "protect" the child-part that acts out (so that the Critic won't have to). The therapist takes an active role as the *wise adult* - the role her father played, and a role that she never felt her mother did as well. The Critic, although still present, has less impact than it used to; and Melissa is becoming more skilled at recognizing her inner critical voice before it becomes destructive and "out of control".

The therapist weaves both models regularly, and each approach plays an indispensable role in helping Melissa move toward very real and concrete change.

The <u>Focusing</u> approach has been essential in allowing Melissa to work through her feelings of worthlessness and abandonment. She is learning that she needs to take full responsibility for managing her Critic, and regularly giving her child-part the kind of time, attention, and empathic caring that somehow got left behind with the death of her father.

The <u>Solution</u> approach has been invaluable in helping Melissa create a picture of what she would like to have happen in her life. Structure and concrete homework provide the tools that help Melissa keep her behavior under control between sessions.

At this writing Melissa has just been promoted again, and has, of her own volition, and without consultation with the therapist, broken off what would have been another destructive relationship. She feels this is the most "adult" step she has taken so far.

PURSUING: A Word to Experiential Psychotherapists

I would like to say a word about *pursuing*. There is no clinical term in either model called "pursuing"; this is my *made-up* word for what is called in the Brief Therapy models "tracking" or "following-through".

For therapists who have been trained in Experiential models, especially the client-centered approaches of Rogers and Gendlin, the act of following-through or tracking is more than challenging - it can initially seem downright painful and anti-intuitive. For the skilled Brief therapist, especially those to whom tracking seems to come so naturally, it is sometimes difficult to understand why this is so hard for Experiential practitioners. In the Brief world it would be something like driving part way; why not follow-through and get to your final destination!

For the experientially trained therapist, tracking can appear at first as too directive, too intrusive, and to the purists in the client-centered community, can seem like something akin to relentless hounding*: Then what?...What then?...What else?* During my own Brief Therapy training I found following-through, or tracking, the most difficult part of the work to master, in spite of the fact that I saw it beautifully and non-intrusively modeled by some brilliant and experienced clinicians.

For me, part of the *solution* to overcoming resistance to tracking and following-through was to revisit my sense of humor. Many Experiential therapists find nothing amusing about (what they perceive as) being directive or intrusive. But the fact is: the process of therapy is not as fragile as some in the experiential world sometimes view it. Indeed, following-through on specific points or goals with clients helps them to see the issues and solutions more clearly.

When the attitude of respecting and valuing the client is present, there is little the therapist can do that will seem disrespectful or offensive. So the word *pursuing* has now become to me a gentle reminder to "lighten up". Hopefully, as the concept of tracking and following-through become more natural for Experiential clinicians, the value in pursuing clients' goals and expectations will become more evident, as you will see in the next intervention, The Miracle Question.

4th INTERVENTION *The Miracle Question*

The Miracle Question was developed by Insoo Kim Berg and Steve de Shazer. It has become legendary in the Brief Therapy world. The therapist suggests the following to the client:

> *Suppose that when you go to sleep tonight, a miracle happens while you are sleeping. Of course, you don't know that a miracle is happening because you are already asleep...but while you are sleeping the problem that brought you here gets totally solved. In the morning you open your eyes, and something seems different. You don't quite know what it is yet, but you can already sense a change. What will be the first thing that you'll notice, that will let you know that a miracle has occurred?*

Notice, in the following examples, how the therapist "follows through" (pursues!) from one question to the next:

A husband and wife are in a marital slump. The wife is the client. The therapist has just asked her the Miracle Question:

> ELLEN: The first thing that would let me know a miracle happened is that I'd give my husband a hug, instead of pretending that I was asleep until he left the room.

> THERAPIST: So that would be really different, giving him a hug instead of pretending you were asleep...What do you think would happen next...?

> ELLEN: He'd give me a hug back.

THERAPIST: Ummm…he'd hug you back. Then what might happen?

ELLEN: Oh, maybe we'd just hold each other for awhile…or if it was the weekend, maybe we'd make love.

THERAPIST So you'd be more affectionate with each other…maybe make love… and what do you imagine might happen after that?

ELLEN: Well, we'd just be more loving…and maybe do things for each other throughout the day.

THERAPIST: That sounds really good…helping each other out more…Anything else that would let you know that a miracle had happened?

ELLEN: Yes…we wouldn't be bickering so much. We'd be more connected…the way we used to be.

THERAPIST: So you'd be more connected…physically and emotionally…and you'd be helping each other out, the way you used to…

ELLEN: Boy, I'd sure like a miracle like that to happen!

The Miracle Question is often followed by Scaling.

THERAPIST: Well, let's just see how close to a miracle you really are. On a scale of one to ten, with ten being the miracle, and one being as bad as it gets, where do you realistically feel it's possible for the two of you to be?

ELLEN: I think if we really worked at it, we could probably be a seven or eight… nothing's perfect, you know…

Bad 1________________**7__8**__10 Miracle

THERAPIST: Very good that you are so realistic...OK, so you could see your relationship as a seven or eight. Where do you think you are on the scale, in your relationship, right now?

ELLEN: Oh, maybe a four or five…some days even a six…

Bad 1______**4**__**5**_____________10 Miracle

THERAPIST: All right, I'm going to mark it down as four to five, even though we know there are times it's even better than that. Now I want to ask you this: What do you think is one small step…just a small one…that would take you from a four to a four and a half, by the next time we meet?

ELLEN: I need to do something about my tone of voice. I can hear myself sounding rude and disrespectful…I don't even say "please" and "thank you" anymore.

THERAPIST: So changing your tone, and speaking in a more respectful way, would be a good first step for you…

ELLEN: If I really did that every day, I think I'd be a solid five…maybe even a five and a half.

THERAPIST: It sounds like that would make a very significant difference in your relationship…changing your tone.

ELLEN: It really would, you know.

THERAPIST: I'm wondering…what kind of difference do you think it would make to your husband…if you were speaking in this new and more respectful way?

ELLEN: Oh huge!…because he talks to me now pretty much the way I talk to him…we're always yapping at each other. I think he'd be more respectful, too.

THERAPIST: Ummm…and how do you think your relationship will be affected… when this new…more respectful tone…happens between the two of you?

ELLEN: I guess we'd start having real conversations again…we don't talk about much of anything, anymore.

THERAPIST: So you'll be having real conversations again…and that will make a big difference in your relationship…

ELLEN: Yes, it will…the big thing is that I think we'd get our sense of humor back…We used to laugh all the time...and we've stopped laughing.

THERAPIST: So that's a big one, being able to laugh and joke with each other again…

ELLEN: This is a very good miracle…I can't wait to go home and try it!

The Miracle Question is a very effective and sometimes playful way to build on concrete steps toward change. It is not an intervention that (some) clinicians will feel comfortable using all the time. If the moment isn't exactly right, it can sound a bit contrived, especially to Experiential therapists. Keep in mind that the same result can be achieved by asking the client:

> *Suppose the problem is solved...What will be the first signs that will let you know that this is no longer a problem?*

The Miracle Question works best when:

- ◊ A change of pace in the session would be helpful.
- ◊ The client actually says: "I could use a miracle, about now!"
- ◊ The client hasn't been able to take the small steps that he or she has agreed to do in previous sessions.
- ◊ The *imagery of a miracle* seems to make a new impact, or different (inner) impression.
- ◊ You are working with children.

Children love miracles and respond with delight to this question. They will often come into a session (if you've used it already) and say, "Can we do another miracle today!"

CASE: CHARLIE

Charlie is 9 years old and going into Grade 4. He is doing poorly at school in spite of the fact that his intelligence is well above average. He is making very little effort; and his parents are concerned, frustrated, and increasingly losing their patience with him.

This is the first session between the therapist and Charlie. The therapist has made several attempts to connect with Charlie, and so far nothing is working: he is not happy to be there and periodically glances at the door.

THERAPIST: It sounds like your schoolwork is giving you a real problem

> The therapist has "externalized" the problem: *He* is not the problem - it is the *schoolwork* that is giving Charlie the problem.

CHARLIE: Yeah…

THERAPIST: And it sounds like your parents and teachers are giving you a problem, too.

CHARLIE: Yeah…

THERAPIST: I guess you'd like to figure out some way to not have this be a problem any more?

CHARLIE: Yeah…

> Given that this session is not exactly moving along with alacrity, the therapist is looking for something *different* to do.

THERAPIST: I have an idea…would you like to imagine something that might be really fun?

CHARLIE: (perks up at the idea that this session could possibly be "fun") Sure!

THERAPIST: OK…how about imagining that when you go to sleep tonight, a *real miracle* happens while you are sleeping. The miracle is that you are doing really well in school. Your homework is done, your parents and teachers aren't bugging you anymore, you can be out playing and having and fun - and you don't have to come here anymore, either.

CHARLIE (some excitement): Well, I sure like the idea of not coming here any more…nothing wrong with you, Ma'am…but I don't think I'm nuts.

THERAPIST: Of course, you're *not nuts,* Charlie…not even close…I just want to help you get your parents off your back…so life will be a bit happier for you…Wanna go back to the miracle? (He nods enthusiastically.) OK...so, you don't know that a miracle is happening because you are sleeping. In the morning you open your eyes, and you know that something *feels different...* you don't quite know what it is yet, but you *just know* that something has changed. What will be the first thing that you'll notice, that will let you know that a miracle has happened?

CHARLIE: The first thing is that I will want to go to school…I mean no one ever really *wants* to go to school…but I mean I won't dread it…I won't just put the covers over my head and pretend that the alarm clock didn't ring…you know what I mean?

THERAPIST: Yes, I think so…it sounds like you're saying that you'd look *a little forward* to going to school, and you'd get out of bed instead of putting the covers over your head…What do you think would happen next?

CHARLIE: Well, I'd get out of bed and get dressed more quickly instead of goofing around for as long as I can.

THERAPIST: I see…and what do you imagine will be different…when you're getting dressed more quickly…and not goofing around?

CHARLIE: Oh, that's easy…my mom wouldn't be yelling at me to hurry up and get dressed…to get down to breakfast so I won't be late.

THERAPIST: So your mom would stop yelling at you to hurry up…

CHARLIE: Yeah…every morning starts with yelling and screaming… It's one of the reasons I hate to get out of bed…

THERAPIST: So when you are getting dressed more quickly…and when your mom isn't yelling at you…what will be the next thing that you'll notice…that tells you that a miracle happened?

CHARLIE: I guess breakfast time would be…what's the word?…

THERAPIST: More pleasant?

CHARLIE: More calm…my mom isn't half bad when she's calm…she can even be kind of cool sometimes…But when she starts yelling…Oh boy, watch out! She really flips out sometimes…

THERAPIST: So in this miracle picture, your mom is calm, you eat your breakfast… Then what would happen?…you know…more signs that would tell you that a miracle had happened…

CHARLIE: I'd get to school, and hand in my homework, no excuses…and the teacher would smile at me instead of giving me that dirty look she has.

THERAPIST: You'd really notice a change in your teacher…and how she treats you…I wonder how that will be…when she's being nicer to you?

CHARLIE: Oh, that look!…it just gives me the creepy jeepies...like a hard ball in my stomach…and then I feel really bad about myself…

THERAPIST: So when you don't do your homework…*things happen*…yelling and dirty looks…that leave you feeling bad about yourself…

CHARLIE: Yeah…I hate that feeling…yuk.

THERAPIST: So it would be really great for you…to be able to get rid of that yukky feeling…and have some more fun…and feel good…

CHARLIE: You ain't just kiddin'!…I mean…that's no joke…

THERAPIST: I want to show you something…(takes out a piece of paper and draws a scale.) Here's a scale from one to ten. Let's pretend that the number ten on the scale is "very good". That means good with your parents, good with your teachers, good grades, feeling good about yourself...OK?...and number one on the scale is "yukky"...bad grades, bad feelings, the whole works.

Yukky 1________________________10 Very good

Where do you think you could really be on the scale? What I mean by "really" is if you don't actually believe you'll ever be a ten…then you want to find a number that fits with what you know you can do.

CHARLIE: I could be a ten.

THERAPIST: Really?

CHARLIE: Yeah…you may not believe this…but school isn't that hard for me…(a bit triumphantly) I could be an A student if I wanted to…

THERAPIST: Ummm…I'm a bit confused…I can't help wondering…well…if you *know* you could be a ten…and if school is really that easy for you…what stops you from doing it?

CHARLIE (very long pause): Well…they did this testing at my school…it's about getting into what they call the "Gifted Program"…and if I do well at school, I'm gonna be in it and…(the story explodes out of him)…Do you have any idea what kind of nerds are in that program! I'd be the laughing stock of all my friends!! Those kids are losers...I'm telling you they are the losers of the planet…and I'll die before I have to go into a program with all those losers…! I just WON'T DO IT!! - I'd rather fail school then be with those nerdy losers…(sobs)… it's just not fair…

THERAPIST (gives him some time to compose himself then says gently): You know, Charlie, it sounds to me like the *real miracle* is that you would do well in school…and be allowed to choose *not* to go into the "Gifted Program".

CHARLIE (with wide-eyed awe): Do you think that is possible?

THERAPIST: I think we should have a talk with your parents and find out.

Comments:

- ◊ Using the Miracle Question turned out to be a vital entry into the real issue, and a way to get Charlie to open up and speak; he was very resistant at the beginning of the session.

- ◊ As it transpired, completing the scaling process became unnecessary. Charlie's clarity about being able to attain a ten on the scale took the session in an entirely different direction.

- ◊ The therapist was touched and amazed at the amount of trouble and aggravation that Charlie was willing to endure to avoid, what looked to him like a "fate worse than death".

- ◊ At a later juncture, the therapist complimented Charlie on his "resourcefulness" in dealing with the problem. Together, the therapist and Charlie explored what might be a better (and less painful) way of dealing with difficult issues in the future.

- ◊ Charlie had been concerned - more accurately, convinced - that his parents, who could not afford an independent private school for their exceptionally bright son, would not consider his point of view. He believed that they saw the Gifted Program as the *only* other option.

- ◊ Through some further work with the whole family, the parents, who were quite impressed that their son had gone to so much trouble to "win his case", agreed to "consult and consider" before "deciding for him" what he should do. They all came to see how important it was to work as a team in *tackling the issue*, rather than having their son *be the issue.* Together, they explored alternative options.

Adapting the Miracle Question Experientially

Focusing Oriented therapists may or may not be attracted to the Miracle Question in its standard form, primarily because the "follow-through" or "tracking" might feel too directive for some. The following example is an adaptation of the Miracle Question and Scaling using a more Experiential approach and tone.

The therapist might begin with some form of guided imagery, to bring the client inside the body:

> *Close your eyes...take a few deep breaths...and take a moment to find a position that is both relaxed...yet aware...and when you feel ready...ask inside...if there is anything that just feels right to work on today?...take your time...and let your body give you the situation or issue, that needs some attention, right now...and let me know when you are ready...*

The client will indicate when s/he has chosen something.

> *Then, imagine...that when you go to sleep tonight...while you are sleeping... a miracle happens, and the issue or problem that is bothering you is solved. You don't know that a miracle is happening because you are sleeping...but it does happen. In the morning, you open your eyes and somehow...something feels different...you can sense it immediately. Can you ask inside: What will be the first thing that will let me know that a miracle has occurred?*

Anita: I think the first thing that will let me know a miracle has happened is that I won't keep procrastinating about things.

Therapist: You'll notice that something about procrastinating...has changed...

Anita: When I wake up...and start to think about all the things I *should* do, I get so bummed out...I just want to stay in bed.

THERAPIST: So you are saying that when the miracle happens…you'll *want* to get out of bed…

ANITA: Yes…I *will* get out of bed…if it really was a miracle I'd leap out of bed…my husband leaps out of bed…I don't know how he does it…

THERAPIST: So when the miracle happens, the first thing you will notice is how you'll leap out of bed…can you *sense*…what might happen next?

ANITA: Ummm…while I'm brushing my teeth and getting dressed, I'll already be thinking about the things that I want to accomplish for the day…like goals…I'm awful about following through on my goals…I make them…but then I just put them off…

The therapist sees that she is about to go off on a tangent about how she *doesn't* stick with her goals, and brings the conversation back to the Miracle Question.

THERAPIST: So while you are getting yourself ready with your morning preparations…you will already be thinking about the things you want to accomplish for the day…and reviewing your goals…Maybe imagine here: what it will *feel like*, being you…preparing, getting organized, thinking things through.

ANITA: Ahhh…it will feel great…I always like myself better when I do what I set out to do.

THERAPIST: That will feel great…you'll be liking yourself better…and feeling good about what you are setting out to do…See what else will let you know that a miracle has happened?

ANITA: I'll write stuff down…you know, make lists…when I just think about stuff I usually forget it about as fast as I think it…and I'm always thinking about something…but when I write it down, it's somehow more…real… yeah, that's it…it's *more real!*

THERAPIST: It's more real, somehow…writing stuff down helps you to remember better...and makes what you want to do seem more real…see if there's more…

ANITA: I would go right to my desk…ugh, my desk…what a disaster area…I don't even know where to start to get my desk organized…just seeing my desk clean would be a miracle…

THERAPIST (stays with the miracle): OK…so cleaning up your desk is a big one… and that goes on the list as something you'd like to do… Check and see… what else you would like to put on your miracle list?

ANITA: Let's see…there's my desk…then…I've been putting off simple things… paying bills…answering some correspondence…you know…just the normal stuff people have to do…

THERAPIST: So it's just stuff…normal stuff that has to be done…

ANITA: Yeah…and I really need to do it…because I have other projects that I really want to do…I need to organize my life...what a mess…

THERAPIST: So…taking the time to get everything down on the list will help you see what you need to do…and in what order.

ANITA: Yeah, it would…and I really feel that if I'd just write stuff down that would help a lot...

THERAPIST: Maybe just check again, and see if there is anything else that wants to come in here…

ANITA: Just that I know that when I am more organized I like myself a whole lot better…and I'm less critical and more accepting of myself.

THERAPIST: Maybe take an extra minute here…to *sense that good feeling* of…less critical and more accepting…liking yourself better…

Anita (takes some quiet time): Ummm…I like the feeling a lot…(loses the feeling) I just don't like doing that kind of desk stuff…it takes up too much time…

Therapist: So there are two things here…one is that you like the good feeling of being more organized, and the other is that you don't want it to take up too much time.

Anita: Yes, that's exactly right…it's so boring…and I have to do it.

Therapist: So let's see if we can break this down into something realistic…that feels doable. Let's imagine that we have a scale ranging from one to ten. Ten would mean being very organized and efficient, managing well with your time and lists; and one would be disorganized and procrastinating. Realistically, where do you see yourself…that is…what do you feel is possible for you, that your *body buys?"*

Anita: This has never been my strong point...I always have to work at it. My husband is like a neat-freak, you know..."anal" I think they call it…

Therapist: OK…this is very important…this isn't about how you can be more like your husband…this is about what *you* feel you can realistically achieve… what it feels like being Anita…doing this stuff…and about how efficient or orderly…whatever you want to call it…

Anita: Organized…

Therapist: Alright, "organized"…it's about how organized you see yourself being…and then…leaving some *space and permission*…for the part of you that will never be like your husband…take a minute here to sense what is real for you…

Anita: My body buys a five…maybe a six on a really good day…beyond that…I can't imagine beyond that, right now.

THERAPIST: And that's just fine…take a minute to let your body know that you would be delighted if it was a five…we won't even deal with six today…just sense how pleased you'd be with a five…

Disorganized 1__________**5**_________10 Organized

ANITA: It buys that…

THERAPIST: Good…now ask yourself: *Where am I on the scale, right now, today?*

ANITA: Ugh…do I really have to tell you!

THERAPIST (laughs): This isn't a test at school, you know…this is you, talking to you…*with some patience!*…just gently…sense where you are…

ANITA: A zero!

THERAPIST: Mmmm…I think you're being a bit tough on yourself…this is about learning how to do something new, in a way that is respectful, over time, that your body buys…small manageable steps…

ANITA: Well…truthfully?…I think I'm probably about a two…

THERAPIST: Will you take a moment to check if a two feels right?

ANITA: Sometimes I'm a one and a half…sometimes two…and on a really good day a two and a half.

THERAPIST: So two is pretty realistic…sometimes a bit less… sometimes better... but two is pretty accurate...

1___**2**__________________10

ANITA: Yeah, I think it actually is.

THERAPIST: See what you can *realistically* do…between now and the next time we meet, *that you buy*, that will take you from a two to a solid two and a half…just one or two concrete things.

ANITA: I'll start making lists…getting things down on paper. I'll start to sort through the mail and bills…maybe I'll just do a portion of my desk...but *not* the whole thing.

THERAPIST: So the desk is something to be really aware of…that sort of stops the process for you…like…if the desk business gets too overwhelming, you feel paralyzed in some way...then you give up. Can you see what needs to happen there for you?

ANITA: I need to give it a time limit…say fifteen minutes…*that's it!*…and then do another fifteen minutes the next day…and accept that it's the best I can do…but not more, or I'll give up on the whole thing.

THERAPIST: So success here…is really around setting reasonable limits… fifteen minutes feels manageable…beyond that is too much…and you feel comfortable with that…yes?

ANITA: Yes, I can manage it…as long as I know that I don't have to do my whole desk…all at one time!

Comments:

The significant factor in helping Anita move forward was giving herself (the part of her that will never be the "neat-freak" that she perceives her husband to be) permission and acceptance regarding her own limits. The truth was that, except for her guilty feelings, she cared far less about being organized, and far more about the other creative aspects of her life; being neat simply was not that important to her.

The challenge with Anita was in helping her find a new balance that her body would *buy:* a realistic view of becoming "somewhat organized", which she wanted, while not becoming overly concerned with being neat, which in fact was not appealing to her at all. She felt that her creativity and spontaneity would be hampered if organization became her raison d'etre. Interestingly, she had no particular interest in pursuing the matter further. Over time she became a mostly contented five on the scale!

The Miracle Question With Groups

The Miracle Question is a very good process-exercise for almost any kind of group work. It can be tailored quite successfully for business groups, school groups, spiritual workshops, people in recovery; and it's a natural for workshops with couples.

It is best practiced in dyads, with each person (person A and person B) taking turns. The group leader guides the whole group through a process-exercise, giving the participants time to sense, *Which issue would be right to work on today?* After the participants pick their issue, partnerships are formed. The group leader then guides the dyads through the Miracle Question, at the end of which the partners take turns working with each other.

Note: it is essential to the smooth working of the exercise, and to avoid taxing the level of expertise of the participants, that the partners are instructed to pick an issue that is manageable - not the hardest, heaviest, most pressing problem they are carrying around!

Print out a simple guide sheet that each partner will use when it is his or her turn to listen. The facilitator can adapt some form of the following:

Asking. The listener asks the speaker:

> *What is the first thing that will let you know that a miracle has happened?*

Listening. Each time the speaker explains what will be happening when a miracle occurs, the listener reflects back what the speaker has said:

> *So the first thing you'll notice is...*

Affirming. When the speaker affirms (or nods) that is what s/he meant, the listener asks:

> *Is there more?*

Each time, the listener reflects back what the speaker has said.

The listener continues with:

- ◊ Anything else…? Or *What else will you be feeling…doing…differently, when you know that a miracle has occurred?*
- ◊ Scaling: When the process comes to a natural end (i.e., when there is nothing further to say about the miracle) scaling can be used to help the speaker measure his or her progress.
- ◊ Time is allowed for sharing. The speaker expresses how s/he felt about the process, and what s/he gained from the experience.
- ◊ Partners switch and after scaling is completed, the listener shares his/her experience.

The **value** of this exercise is three-fold:

- ◊ First, the specificity of the question, *What exactly will be happening when the miracle occurs?* brings the participants closer to their goals and aspirations.
- ◊ Second, they learn how to use the miracle question without the help of a facilitator (another way to feel more empowered).
- ◊ Finally, the partners have an opportunity to share in a creative and often meaningful way.

Because it is a miracle, they experience a kind of magical quality that allows for the creative imagination to blossom and soar; the participants can imagine anything, with no restrictions - because, after all, it is a miracle!

Focusing - Solution Style

EXERCISE: Getting inspiration from someone you admire

The following exercise has been very useful in helping individuals, clients, or groups to measure their self-esteem. This exercise also works particularly well in business settings. Feel free to adapt it in any way that will fit.

First, guide the person or group into an inner, quiet space, then continue with imagery...

Imagine someone that you admire and respect...someone you value and look up to...Now imagine being with this person and notice…where you are…what time of day it is…and what you are doing together...

Notice…how you feel in their presence…taking time to sense…what is it that you *experience inside*…what you *feel*…when you are with this person…

See…if a word or image comes, that exactly describes what you *sense* is the essential quality of this person. Then ask yourself, *What is it about him or her that makes me feel this way?* Notice the quality word, or image, that just exactly describes what being with this person *does inside of you*...take a minute to let that form…

If something comes…take a moment to fully *have it inside...*

Then ask yourself, *What part of this person…their essential quality…do I want to be more like?...or have more of...for myself?* (e.g. empathy, courage, patience, creativity, assertiveness)…

Imagine a scale from one to ten. Ten represents the very best of that quality, and one, not having that quality at all.

Ask yourself, *Where on the scale would I realistically like to be?* Then check… where you are on the scale in your life, right now?

Next, ask yourself, *What is one small thing, a small action step that I can do that would bring me up one half point on the scale…then sense…*

◊ What you will feel, be like, look like, when you are doing that small step?

◊ Who is the very first person you will want to share this with?…do more of *this with…?*

◊ *How will that person be with you…when you've made those changes?*

◊ *Where…in what circumstances…will you want to try doing this, first?*

Find a symbol, word, or feeling, that will help you remember this action step later on…tomorrow…in a few weeks from now…and ask inside for a way that will help you remember this symbol, word, or feeling, so that you can access them anytime you want to...

Then try a little review to see if you remember…Imagine being with someone and doing the old behavior…the exact opposite of the quality you have chosen (e.g. impatience, weakness, etc)… Suddenly, you remember the symbol, word or feeling that helps you remember where you want to be on the scale. Try it on…in this moment…and notice how you change…your attitude, words, body language, and inner feeling...when you remember…how it will be when it's just right…

Take some time here to fully *receive*…whatever came…knowing that *you will remember* this...and can come back to it *again and again*...whenever *you want to...* Remind yourself of how wonderful this quality *looks and feels on you!*

Finally, just before the process ends, make a note to yourself…each time you feel comfortable and stable with a new half point on the scale, you can repeat this process asking again…

◊ Where *am I on the scale right now?*

◊ Where would I like to be?

◊ What small step can I take that will bring me to the next half point…to *reach my desired goal on the scale?*

The Wrap-up: Review

Have something to say; say it; and stop when you're done.

Tyrone Edwards

Where Focusing Oriented and Experiential models work best:

◊ Exposing clients to the act of processing: experiencing the *bodily felt-sense* of an issue, and taking the necessary time to learn how to *keep company* with inner feelings.

◊ Exposing clients to the language and friendly *attitude* (the "Focusing Attitude") toward the Self: safety; inner space; *making room for* places that are hurting, negative, stuck; non-judgment; permitting and allowing whatever feelings come, to *just be there.*

◊ Giving clients an awareness of inner parts: Critic, inner child, and Self.

◊ Learning how to listen: internally to the Self and externally to others.

◊ Psycho-education: teaching clients explicitly more about their process.

Where Solution Oriented and Brief Therapy models work best:

◊ Interrupting patterns:

- Helping the client break out of old, negative patterns and behaviors that are so embedded the client doesn't notice they are there.

- Helping clients learn how to *do something different.*

◊ Creating change by learning how to consciously re-construct problems and issues into positive new realities (the Solution Picture) that *are* and *feel* different, fresh, and new.

◊ Managing overwhelming and uncontrollable feelings that impede clear thinking and creative intelligence.

◊ Creating more options when time and/or funds are limited for pursuing long-term therapy.

◊ Shifting attention away from what doesn't work into to *what is possible.*

INTEGRATING BOTH

What the Focusing Oriented model gives to the Solution approach:

◊ Knowledge, awareness and grounding in the *experience of processing;* taking time to explore the *felt-sense* of an issue.

◊ Time and permission to work with what *doesn't work,* what's wrong (instead of what would be right); resistance, negativity and stuck places.

What the Solution Oriented model gives to the Focusing approach:

◊ Directionality, purpose, intention, and better understanding of what exactly the client *can* and *will* do to create positive change.

◊ A structure to diminish affect (when the intensity of emotion blocks the process of moving forward) by adding cognitive and behavioral components.

Focusing

The beauty of the Focusing Oriented model is in its gentleness, respectfulness, and explicit teaching of an *attitude* toward the Self that is caring, empathic, willing to listen, and most of all *values all parts* of the Self. The Focusing Oriented model permits and allows whatever wants to unfold to do so, in a safe and nurturing inner environment that promotes healing and growth. Focusing honors the wisdom of the felt-sense, and works actively with various parts in order to integrate them into the whole.

Solution

The beauty of the Solution Oriented model is in its respectful, positive attitude and non-problem-oriented approach. The model provides a safe structure in which to explore and create new, more constructive possibilities, with consequent alternative behaviors. The skillful use of language allows clients to access, in a time-efficient manner, what they *do want*, rather than what they don't want.

SOFT: making room for both

My purpose in writing this book was to share something that deeply excites me a) because it's clear to me that *it works!* and b) because I see the excitement in my clients as they recognize their own changes and improvements. The usual comments from them are either, *"Wow, what a great question! I've never even thought of that before..."* or *"What a difference it made to really spend some time with that. I've never really done that before..."*

It seems to me that there is *'something'* that is natural and organic in partnering or marrying BOTH the Experiential and Brief approaches to our therapy work. I hope you will find (as I have) that this weaving together enhances each model in valuable and concrete ways.

Integrating Experiential and Brief Therapy allows for an expanded advantage to both the therapist and client. *SOFT* is the intricate and subtle weaving and blending of:

◊ The gentle process of Focusing with a Solution Orientation

and/or

◊ The respectful process of Solution work with a Focusing Orientation.

Either way, the resulting experience for clients is an increased awareness of *Self* and *other*, enhanced by a new sense of *felt*-hopefulness: finding manageable solutions to seemingly impossible situations.

The Integrated Therapist: Final Thoughts for Clinicians

As I come to a close, a thought occurs to me. I have said a lot here about integrating Experiential and Brief Therapy. Now I would like to say a closing word about *The Integrated Therapist.*

Our diversity as practitioners is a given. Each of us takes new material and according to our natural modalities and processing styles, internalizes (what might be exactly the same data) in vastly different ways. Some clinicians will have a natural inclination for experiential work, and within that school, some will lean even further in the direction of pure, non-directive client-centered therapy. Others will be totally comfortable with directional, goal setting approaches. The so-called 'weavers' will find themselves somewhere in the middle, using a combination of both, at different junctures. In the end, the Integrated Therapist is one who can adapt to whatever circumstances present themselves in the therapy room (and in life, for that matter!)

When the clinician is comfortable and working in a way that is in alignment with who and how s/he intrinsically is - anything can work! Here are the essential basics that represent (what I feel/view) as the foundational elements for all clinical work:

◊ Relationship: To quote Rogers, an attitude of "unconditional positive regard" and "empathy" are the keys to *right relationship* in the therapy room. It is the relational aspect that allows a client to feel valued, respected, cared about, and understood. We know that therapeutic relationships vary with each person. With some, we feel closer and more connected, with others more distant. Whatever the relationship may be (connected, unique or even peculiar) the client needs to feel that s/he can speak openly and freely – in the end having the experience of feeling genuinely understood.

◊ Safety: The client is able to open up interiorly, no matter what the content of his/her issue, without feeling judged, belittled, or scrutinized. Said another way, the clinician is able to separate the dysfunction from the person (no matter how troublesome the dysfunction may be).

◊ Congruence: The therapist is practicing in a way that 'fits' his/her natural style and way of being. For some, aspects such as 'self disclosure' or 'therapist's use of self' will feel comfortable. Others will prefer a more neutral stance. It doesn't matter as long as the clinician feels s/he is operating out of genuine authenticity.

◊ Processing: Ability of the therapist to help clients *process* (in some form). As we have seen, some clients are naturally process-oriented and others are not. There is, however, a way (whether the dialogue is an inward reflection with self or a conversation with the therapist) that clients can be gently coached to speak from authenticity, in the moment, rather than from cognitive memory or 'shoulds'.

I believe that the basic requirements for clients to experience change are:

- the ability to access some level of authenticity or genuine Self
- the ability to sense genuine *wants* and *needs*
- genuine willingness to do the work (with support from the therapist)

With the above points in place, all doors are open…

As is beautifully stated in Ecclesiastes:

> *"To every thing there is a season, and a time…"*

So to you, dear Reader, my sincere hope that you will find the right time and season for each orientation, in its rightful place.

But What About...
Frequently Asked Questions

The following questions have been asked often enough that I thought it might be valuable to devote an entire section to them. (These questions have been transcribed from numerous workshops that I have presented over the years.)

QUESTION: *About the four Interventions that you mentioned...do you have to use all of them in each session?*

RESPONSE: Thank you for asking that. No, you don't. Each of them is useful at different times - different junctures. They are there for the taking - use them when they seem relevant.

QUESTION: *How brief is Brief?*

RESPONSE: That's a great question. I'm afraid my answer may be less brief than your question! (laughter)

The term "Brief" has certainly undergone an evolution over the years. Originally, Brief Therapy was devised to cope with the constraints of Managed Care and short-term Health Insurance for psychotherapy. Therapy ranged anywhere from four to eight sessions, and was designed to get the best possible results in the shortest period of time. The Brief Therapy models were efficient and effective. They addressed clearly and simply the questions of: *What is the issue? What do you want to have happen? How can we help you get there?*

Over the years, however, there has been an interesting shift in attitude toward Brief Therapy as more and more clinicians have become familiar with its various adaptations. The depth and integrity of Brief Therapy has stood the test of time, and the effectiveness of the approach has continued to make so much therapeutic sense.

Brief Therapy's specificity of language, and its special way of phrasing questions, has produced wonderful insights, as well as answers, for patients. And, many clinicians began treating the Brief Therapy models (such as the Solution Focused Therapy of Berg and de Shazer) as an orientation and a style of working - not just as a way to save time.

So "Brief" doesn't necessarily mean brief anymore. The various Brief Therapy models may be short-term, but when integrated into other models, as I hope I have demonstrated, the work may easily cover long-term therapy that simply embraces a Solution Oriented style - or parts of it anyway.

QUESTION: *You mentioned the use of language...and earlier talked about being "bi-lingual". Does the mixing of language ever get confusing?*

RESPONSE: Not any more, but it used to, since experiential language came first – it's my "mother tongue", so to speak. The experiential way of phrasing includes a very specific – *in its vague way* (laughter!) – style of speaking. It is ever tentative, with lots of dot…dot…dots…to a) enhance the clients' *felt* response and b) to allow clients to *grope* for exactly the right word that fits their direct experience. Also, there is the emphasis on making *gentle suggestions,* rather than asking *direct questions,* which of course the Solution model does all the time. I remember during my Brief Therapy training, bursting into laughter, while I was fumbling around trying to get the language right: "What do *you* imagine *she* would say *you* could do that would be helpful to *her?"* It just drove me crazy and I got it wrong at least half of the time!

But I know something now that I didn't quite realize then; and it may be useful for you. Did you ever learn to ride a bike? Or drive a stick shift-car? You can't do it…and you can't do it…and then suddenly you *can* - something just kicks in! And what that is, is moving from *cognitive understanding* to direct *inner knowing.* Your body will remember how to ride a bike or drive the stick-shift car even if you haven't done it for twenty years. Why? Because the knowing has been *internalized.*

So my suggestion is this: If the Solution language is new to you, then get very quiet as you study it, and try to internalize the *meaning* behind the words - so you get a *felt experience* of the Solution language that makes sense…and resonates with your whole being.

Here's another suggestion. Most Brief Therapists have learned to be quite masterful (with the use of language). Those less familiar (with the linguistic style) will find it very worthwhile to study Jay Haley's work on Milton Erickson, and also the many books on Neuro-Linguistic Programming (NLP) by Bandler and Grinder, and by Connirae and Steve Andreas. The linguistic techniques, the intricacies of phrasing, and the effects of language on the psyche are clearly explained, with excellent case examples.

QUESTION: *Still on this same point about language...can you do it wrong?*

RESPONSE: Rarely. The client will let you know. They'll say: *"I'm not sure what you mean"* or *"I didn't get that."* One of my favorite Gendlin lines is: *"The wronger you get it, the righter they will get it!"* And that's so true because the client is forced...(laughs) ...Gendlin would never use the word "force"!...Anyway, your *lack of understanding* will help *increase* the *client's understanding,* bringing them closer to figuring out what they mean...especially through their trying to explain it to you!

QUESTION: *This is about the model you demonstrated for dialoguing. When the patient takes on the role of...let's say his partner...is he always accurate in what his partner will say? I mean...does it ever happen that the person twists around the words of what the other might say...so that they are not exactly speaking the truth?*

RESPONSE: Never! Or at least not in my experience and I'll tell you why. The client *wants* you to hear what his "other half" has to say (we'll say *he* for now). Why? He wants to pour out his story and he wants me to hear *his* side. Then he wants me to hear *her* side. It isn't as if he's hiding what she's going to say...he wants me to know her side and he wants to be accurate about it...because he thinks he's going to prove to me that *he's right* and *she's wrong!* (laughter)

QUESTION: *But do they really know what their partner would say?*

RESPONSE: Have you ever worked with children? Have you ever asked a kid, "What would your mother say about that...(x)...behavior...?" And the kid has got it down verbatim: *"Ugghhhh, yeah...my mom, she always says..."* The kid has heard this so many times it's become totally internalized.

So the client can tell you verbatim what his wife would say. He always knows, just like the kid knows. It's nothing new. He lives with the same conversations all the time; he knows them inside out and backward.

QUESTION: *Still on this same point. Does the husband ever feel unsafe? For instance, either you might side with the wife, or maybe he'll feel exposed by having her say things like, "He's abandoned me".*

RESPONSE: I very carefully construct how the dialogue will take place, making a clear distinction between my interactions with her and with him. Then I do several things:

First, I ask his permission, to make sure it's OK that I speak with his (absent) spouse.

Second, I turn my chair a bit toward *her.* That seems like such a small thing, but it creates an impression for him that his space is safe, because I'm with *her*, right now.

Third, I never challenge him or turn back to him while I am speaking with her, so that he won't feel as if he has to defend himself against what she is saying. When I'm ready to speak with him again, I slightly turn the chair or my body back toward him, to give him a quick psychological moment to readjust to my direct interaction with him.

Lastly, I'm not trying to "trip him up". I'm genuinely attempting to help him see both sides; and hopefully, through some skillful questions, I can gently lead him toward a different or wider perspective.

QUESTION: *My training is in client-centered therapy, and frankly, no offense intended, I've avoided this work because it seems overly directive to me, and I am uncomfortable with that.*

RESPONSE: I want to be very careful in how I respond to your question, because I don't want to create the impression that I am trying to *convince* you of anything. This is not a religion, and I'm not a Holy Roller, with some message about having "Found the Way". I really mean that.

So, maybe I can just share some of my personal experience with you, and for all of you who come from a client-centered perspective…sit with it…see if any parts of it fit…and use whatever *feels right* to you.

My training was initially client-centered as well, and I frankly had similar concerns when I started. In fact, I was so nervous that my colleagues in the Focusing community - especially Gendlin - would be so horrified at what I was doing that I actually kept it a secret for a couple of years, fearing that if they knew what I was doing maybe they'd throw me out!

I have to laugh at that now. When I presented this *SOFT* approach for the first time at a Focusing International Conference, I discovered that a huge number of my colleagues were already into the Solution work as well; and they had gone into it with exactly the same reservations I had. So we all sort of, pardon the expression, "came out of the closet" together!

So, this is what I have learned: *Attitude, attitude, attitude*. Even Gendlin says that when you bring a caring presence, empathy, and real concern for the client into your work, there's not very much you can do wrong. Add really good listening skills and the genuine desire to serve - which is why we're all doing what we do, anyway - and how far off can you possibly go?

QUESTION (same speaker): *Yes, but what about…what strikes me as being so manipulative?*

RESPONSE: I don't like the word manipulative either. But if we go back to the term "right attitude" then the Solution work doesn't feel like manipulation. The operative word here is "strategies", and I don't mind that term at all. The Solution work has many wonderful strategies that really do work in facilitating positive change. It seems totally plausible to me that a clinician can use a strategy *and* be respectful at the same time, again, the famous *Both/And*. Also, because I wanted to serve people who sometimes had time and/or financial constraints, I felt a need to find something that could move clients more quickly to defining and taking "action steps"; I found that a Solution orientation complemented the Experiential work seamlessly. I can't say it enough: it's not an *either/or*, but a *both/and*.

Finally, we learn new things all the time. The bottom line in being a really good clinician is to take what you learn, internalize it, and make it your own so that it comes out authentically…in your style, with your special way of speaking and relating to your clients. The work has to have, if this is the right way to say it, *your signature* on it.

QUESTION: *I'm still not clear about when you use the Solution approach with couples, and when you use the Focusing or Experiential approach.*

RESPONSE: This is a great question and again, it's a both/and, not either/or. Let's break this down a bit for clarity.

I find the Solution approach so truly effective for difficult couples. I love the structure of the work, and the model helps me to keep really argumentative couples from spinning out of control.

I feel however, that there is a point in the therapy process where couples (or family members or co-workers) need to learn how to *listen to* and *hear* each other, how to experience what the other person is saying, and how to *sense the impact* that their own words and actions have on the other person. In this regard the Interactive Focusing Process works wonderfully.

That said, what I do now is so integrated, so woven together, it's hard to separate the elements. For example, I might ask a male client a Solution question like: "What is one thing that your wife can do that will be helpful to you in the next week?" And maybe he says, "I'd like her to use more encouraging and less critical language. I'd like to be acknowledged for what I do right, instead of always hearing what I do wrong." Right in that spot I might add an experiential piece by asking: "Can you let her know how that would *make you feel…*when she is doing that?" After he expresses his feelings I might turn to her and ask: "How does that *sit inside of you?...* knowing that he carries this sense of always feeling so put down." After awhile, when they've both expressed their feelings, I'll probably get back on a Solution track, pinning down what they need to do that *will work* until the next session.

Again, it is so important for each of you to sense what comes naturally to you and your clients, and to keep experimenting. The Solution model is ideal to get away from the "problems" and work toward something better. The Focusing model is ideal to make sure that clients are internalizing the work so that their *bodies remember* it, even if they don't!

QUESTION: *Do you work with children, and if so, which model works best?*

RESPONSE: Great question, thanks. It's a *both/and* again. The Solution model really works well with children, especially when you *externalize* the issue: *How will it be for you when "trouble" is no longer giving you a problem?*

Children like to be active participants in the change process: "What do you think *you* can do that will help?" and imagining, "*Who else* will notice?" It's a little like a game, and they are delighted with themselves when they *know* what's right and feel they can do something about it.

Children also love to visualize and imagine, so the Miracle Question is a really helpful tool as well. Further, if a child is resistant and wanting to get the session over with as quickly as possible, being solution-focused, rather than problem-focused is very helpful.

At the same time, children need to feel heard, understood, and valued. In that department nothing works quite like Experiential Listening, especially when a child needs to tell his or her story. So weaving both models together is really what works best for me.

QUESTION: *The question of time is an issue for me. How much time, in terms of patient contact, do you need to bring in Focusing and then integrate it with the Solution approach? I know this is a longish question but I'm trying to understand if you need to move more rapidly...if you're under the time constraints of a Managed Care case, or the client doesn't have the resources...how you manage time for both models?*

RESPONSE: Let me try to break this question down into parts:

First, when I already know that there will be time and/or financial constraints, I'm probably thinking Solution. However, I also need to take into account the *natural style* of the client. Some people come in, and they are so sensitive and connected already, I don't need to worry about teaching *being in the* body. They are *already there*...so bringing in experiential language, and framing the questions with an orientation towards solutions is an easy thing to do.

On the other hand, if the client doesn't seem to have…let's call it an *experiential aptitude*…I'll probably steer the session toward a Solution approach, and do less experiential-type processing. However, and this is important, I am *always checking* for congruency…to make sure that what the client is saying s/he wants fits with his/her willingness and ability to follow through. Otherwise I'm actually wasting time.

So here's another part: it's about *time.* I don't know if any of you have ever studied any form of Eastern Philosophy (a lot of affirmative head-shakes and nods). One of the principle tenets concerns the concept of "illusion". It goes something like this:

Although a thing may *"appear"* some way, it is actually not that way at all - it's an *"illusion"*. For example, how many of your parents said to you accusingly, *"Do you ever think about anything but yourself?"* (lots of hands and sheepish grins!) But in Eastern traditions, the self is presented with a big capital 'S': the Self (meaning Soul or Higher Self). So in *that* context it would be correct to answer:

"Yes, I most certainly think about my Self, first and foremost. In fact, I think about my Self all the time! Do you know why? Because when I do that, I am aligned, attuned, and in harmony with the universe…and when I feel so centered and at peace, I'm totally available to serve others!"

Can you see what a paradox that is? What is true is just the opposite of what it "appears" to be!

So, with this question of time: the illusion is, *I don't have time to be reflective, or to spend time alone, or to meditate.* But the truth is, I don't have time *NOT to!* I don't have time to make stupid mistakes. I don't have time to clean up the stupid mistakes that could have been avoided in the first place! - if I'd just initially taken some reflective time to simply 'sit with it'.

So I'm suggesting that sometimes *taking* time *saves* time, if you know what I mean. You can say, *"Oh well…Managed Care…I don't have the time for all this experiential stuff."* Or, *"Oh, they only give me six sessions…I don't have the time to fit this in."* But in the two minutes it takes to ask your client to get quiet and tuned-in before a session, or the five minutes it takes for someone to stop, and *sense*, and maybe have a real *Ah ha!* (which is another way of saying *felt-shift*) you may wind up saving a whole session worth of time!

QUESTION: *I am a medical doctor in family practice. While I only do a limited amount of psychotherapy, I certainly do talk with my patients. Any particular applications of this work you might suggest?*

RESPONSE: Good timing for this question. The Focusing Institute has begun creating mini Focusing Protocols for physicians on how they can save time in the long run by using even small bits of Focusing during their patient appointments. Dr. Joan Klagsbrun is orchestrating this project. Here are a few pieces from her work with physicians:

◊ For the patient who has too many issues to deal with in one appointment the doctor might ask:

  We probably won't have time today to cover all of your concerns, so can you just take a moment to sense...what the most important issues are for you today, so you can prioritize them.

  This suggestion assumes time limits and empowers the patient to select at the start of the appointment how to best use the time.

◊ If the doctor has to give out bad news he or she can empathize by saying something like:

  I see that you are feeling disappointed about the results of your test.

  This statement lets the patient know they are understood.

◊ Before giving a nervous patient an injection, the doctor might suggest:

  Take a moment and then you can let me know when you are ready to begin.

  This is so simple, yet it helps the patient to feel more in charge.

◊ If the case will require dealing with ongoing medical care the doctor might ask:

  How can we work together on this? Check and see what you feel you need...and how I can help...

Do you see how important and empowering these simple questions are? The subtle change in approach, especially in regard to the patient feeling heard and consequently cared about, will likely increase patient compliance, and in the long-run, save time for the physician.

QUESTION: *In your experience, have you found that one model or the other is more effective for specific disorders: depression, panic attacks, bi-polar disorder, etc.? It's not going to be a "one size fits all", I don't think.*

RESPONSE: That's really the answer right there, isn't it - one size doesn't fit all. That's exactly why being bi-lingual (or multi-lingual) is so important; you have a lot more options. If you speak to any experienced clinician, they will tell you how they have successfully worked with these disorders, using their own preferred model.

For example, with a panic attack, in one instance it may feel right to ask: *What will it be like when the panic attack isn't happening? When was the last time you successfully managed a panic attack? What were you doing then that worked?* and *How can you do that again?*

In another instance it may feel more right to listen to the *part* that feels so panicky, and then examine the person's *relationship* to the part that has to carry all that panic around. Maybe that part needs to speak, maybe it feels abandoned and alone, maybe it feels beaten up by the Critic. Maybe the client needs to find out, *"If the panic could speak what would it want to say?"* or *"What would it want me to know?"*

What approach each clinician uses has so much to do with natural style and intuition. When a client comes in for the first time, I have no idea what I am going to do. Some clients come in and are very much in touch with what they are talking about. Others come in and can talk about the issue, but are out of touch with - not in a "right relationship" with what they are talking about. I don't know of any other approach that pays as much attention to this idea of "right relationship" with an issue as the Focusing work does; and frankly (to tie this back in with the last question), whatever time it takes to communicate about it seems to save time in the end.

QUESTION: *In the case of the man who had that terrible accident with the machine, was there a reason that you didn't use the Miracle Question? It sure sounded like he needed one.*

Response: Wonderful question, thank you. You know the expression "There's a time and place for everything"? It wasn't the right time or place. I don't feel we would have accomplished anything with the Miracle Question in the first session, and frankly, I wouldn't have touched it with a "ten-foot pole!"

What could he have said? If a miracle happened, *"I'd get out of bed and feel great; there would never have been an accident; I wouldn't worry about money; my wife wouldn't have died, and we'd have retired to Arizona on my pension."* Do you see what I'm getting at? It would have turned into a trip down bad-memory-lane. That may come later, but in the first session I was less interested in finding a miracle than making a *genuine connection.* For me, and this is my intuitive professional judgment call, the gap - or maybe *abyss* is a better word - between his depression and the miracle was too much…almost like…trying to find a solution would have been, in some way, minimizing the issue.

I wanted to bridge the gap with listening, empathy, and most important to me, a connection between us, so he would trust me…and feel that I *got it,* and that I understood how terrible it all was for him.

I was hoping to just simply help him navigate to a place where he could feel anything even remotely like hope…where he could get some glimmer of… *maybe it is possible that it will be OK*…or have some connection with "pro-life" energy or "fresh air". Getting him to where he could say, *"I'm alive and maybe I do have something going for me…"* or *"Yes, I can…"* is already taking him on the road to solutions.

What actually made the biggest impression on him was something I learned from Gene Gendlin: *"IT NEVER SHOULD HAVE HAPPENED!"* It is so crucial to affirm and acknowledge to clients who have suffered from trauma or abuse that *"It's not your fault."* That's the real miracle, you know, when they can grasp that.

Our time is coming to an end. Let me end by repeating one of my favorite expressions: *"There is a time and place for everything."* I sincerely hope that you will find the right times…and places…to experiment creatively with the many possibilities and options of the SOFT approach.

And thank YOU for listening!

References: Brief Therapy

Berg, I. (1991). *Family Preservation: A Brief Workbook*. London: BT Press.

Berg, I., & Miller, S. (1992). *Working with the Problem Drinker: A Solution-Focused Approach.* New York: W.W. Norton.

Cade, B. & O'Hanlon, W.H. (1993). *A Brief Guide to Brief Therapy*. New York: W.W. Norton.

de Shazer, S. (1985). *Keys to Solution in Brief Therapy.* New York: W.W. Norton.

de Shazer, S. (1988). *Clues: Investigating Solutions in Brief Therapy.* New York: W.W. Norton.

de Shazer, S. (1991). *Putting Difference to Work.* New York: W.W. Norton.

Dolan, Y. (1992). *Resolving Sexual Abuse: Solution Focused Therapy and Ericksonian Hypnosis for Adult Survivors.* New York: W.W. Norton.

Fisch, R., Weakland, J., & Segal, L. (1982). *The Tactics of Change: Doing Therapy Briefly.* San Francisco: Jossey-Bass.

Fisher, R., & Ury, W. (1981). *Getting To Yes: Negotiating Agreement Without Giving In.* New York: Penguin.

Gilligan, S., & Price, R. (Eds.). (1993). *Therapeutic Conversations.* New York: W.W. Norton.

Goldner, V. (1992). Making Room for Both/And. *Family Therapy Networker.* March/April, pp. 55-61.

Haley, J. (1963). *Strategies of Psychotherapy*. New York: Grune & Stratton.

Haley, J. (1967a). Toward a Theory of Pathological Systems. In G. H. Zuk & I. Boszormeny-Nagy (Eds.), *Family therapy and Disturbed Families* (pp. 11-27). Palo Alto, CA: Science and Behavior Books.

Haley, J. (Ed.). (1967b). *Advanced Techniques of Hypnosis and Therapy: Selected Papers of Milton H. Erickson.* New York: Grune & Stratton.

Haley, J. (1973). *Uncommon Therapy: The Psychiatric Techniques of Milton H. Erickson.* New York: Norton.

Haley, J. (1976). *Problem-Solving Therapy.* San Francisco: Jossey-Bass.

Haley, J. (Ed.). (1985). *Conversations with Milton H. Erickson, M.D.* New York: Triangle Press.

Imber-Black, E. (1988). *Families and Larger Systems.* New York: Guilford Press.

Jackson, D. D. (1975). The Question of Family Homeostasis. *Psychiatric Quarterly Supplement, 31:* 79-80.

King, E. (1998). Role of Affect and the Emotional Context in Solution-Focused Therapy. *Journal of Systemic Therapies,* Vol. 17:2, pp. 51-64.

Lipschik, E. (1994). The Rush to be Brief. *The Networker.* March/April, pp. 35-39.

Madanes, C. (1981). *Strategic Family Therapy.* San Francisco: Jossey-Bass.

Minuchin, S. (1978). *Families and Family Therapy.* Cambridge, MA: Harvard University Press.

Minuchin, S., & Fishman, H.C. (1981). *Family Therapy Techniques.* Cambridge, MA: Harvard University Press.

Nichols, M. (1984). *Family Therapy Concepts and Methods.* New York: Gardiner Press.

O'Hanlon, W.H. (1987). *Taproots: Underlying Principles of Milton H. Erickson's Therapy and Hypnosis.* New York: W.W. Norton.

O'Hanlon, W.H., & Weiner-Davis, M. (1989). *In Search of Solutions: A New Direction in Psychotherapy.* New York: W.W. Norton.

O'Hanlon, W.H. (1990). A Grand Unified Theory of Brief Therapy: Putting Problems in Context. In J.K. Zeig & S.G. Gilligan (Eds.), *Brief Therapy: Myths, Methods, and Metaphors* (pp. 78-89). New York: Brunner/Mazel.

O'Hanlon-Hudson, P. & O'Hanlon, W.H. (1993). *Rewriting Love Stories: Brief Marital Therapy.* New York: W.W. Norton.

O'Hanlon, W. (1994). The Third Wave. *Family Therapy Networker.* Nov/Dec, pp. 19-29.

O'Hanlon, W. (1997). *A Guide to Possibility Land.* New York: W.W. Norton.

Selvini-Palazzoli, M., Boscolo, L., Cecchin, G. & Prata, G. (1978). *Paradox & Counterparadox.* New York: Jason Aronson.

Selvini-Palazzoli, M., Boscolo, L., Cecchin, G. & Prata, G. (1980). Hypothesizing, Circularity, & Neutrality: Three Guidelines for the Conductor of an Interview. *Family Process,* Vol. 19, pp. 3-12.

Turnell, A. & Lipchik, E. (1999). The Role of Empathy in Brief Therapy: The Overlooked But Vital Context. *Australia New Zealand Journal of Family Therapy,* Vol. 20:4, pp. 177-182.

Walter J., & Peller, J. (1988). Going Beyond the Attempted Solution: A Couple's Meta-Solution. *Family Therapy Case Studies,* Vol. 3, No. 1, pp. 41-45.

Walter, J., & Peller, J. (1992). *Becoming Solution-Focused in Brief Therapy.* New York: Brunner/Mazel.

Watzlawick, P., Beavin, J.H., & Jackson, D.D. (1967). *Pragmatics of Human Communication: A Study of Interactional Patterns, Pathologies, and Paradoxes.* New York: W.W. Norton.

Watzlawick, P., Weakland, J., & Fisch, R. (1974). *Change: Principles of Problem Formation and Problem Resolution.* New York: W.W. Norton.

Watzlawick, P. (1983). *The Situation Is Hopeless, But Not Serious.* New York: W.W. Norton.

Weakland, J.H., Fisch, R., Watzlawick, P., & Bodin, A. (1974). Brief Therapy: Focused Problem Resolution. *Family Process,* Vol. 13, pp. 141-168.

Webster's Dictionary for Everyday Use. (1981). Baltimore: Ottenheimer.

Weiner-Davis, M., de Shazer, S., & Gingerich, W. (1987). Building on Pretreatment Change to Construct the Therapeutic Solution: An Exploratory Study. *Journal of Marital and Family Therapy, 13*(4), pp. 359-363.

Weiner-Davis, M. (1992). *Divorce Busting.* New York: Simon & Schuster.

White, M. (1986). Restraint, and Double Description: A Template for Family Therapy. *Family Process.* June. Vol. 25, No. 2.

White, M. (1988). The Externalizing of the Problem and the Re-Authoring of Lives and Relationships. *Dulwich Centre Newsletter,* Summer: 3-21

White, M., & Epston, D. (1990). *Narrative Means to Therapeutic Ends.* New York: W.W. Norton.

Zeig, J. (1980). *A Teaching Seminar with Milton H. Erickson, M.D.* New York: Brunner/Mazel.

Zeig, J. (1994). *Ericksonian Methods: The Essence of the Story.* New York: Brunner/Mazel.

References: Eperiential Psychotherapy

Assagioli, R. (1975). *Psychosynthesis.* London: Turnstone Books.

Boukydis, C.F.Z. (1990). Client-Centered/Experiential Practice with Parents and Infants. In G. Lietaer, J. Rombauts, & R. Van Balen (Eds.), *Client-Centered and Experiential Psychotherapy in the Nineties.* Leuven, Belgium: Leuven University Press.

Buber, M. (1958). *I and Thou.* New York: Charles Scribner and Sons.

Campbell, P. A., & McMahon, E.M. (1985). *Biospirituality: Focusing As A Way to Grow.* Chicago: Loyola University Press.

Gendlin, E.T. (1962). *Experiencing and the Creation of Meaning.* New York: Free Press. (Reprinted by Macmillan, 1970).

Gendlin, E.T. (1968). The Experiential Response. In E. Hammer (Ed.), *Use of Interpretation in Treatment,* pp. 208-227. New York: Grune & Stratton.

Gendlin, E.T. (1978). *Focusing.* New York: Bantam Books.

Gendlin, E.T. (1984). The Client's Client. In J.M. Shlien, & R. Levant (Eds.), *Client Centered Therapy and the Person-Centered Approach.* New York: Praeger.

Gendlin, E.T. (1986). *Let Your Body Interpret Your Dreams.* Ilinois: Chiron.

Gendlin, E.T. (1996). *Focusing-Oriented Psychotherapy.* New York: Guilford Press.

Greenberg, L.S. & Safran, J. (1987). *Emotion in Psychotherapy: Affect, Cognition, and the Process of Change.* New York: Guilford Press.

Greenberg, L.S. & Johnson, S.M. (1988). *Emotionally Focused Therapy for Couples.* New York: Guilford Press.

Greenberg, L.S., Rice, L.N., & Elliot, R. (1993). *Facilitating Emotional Change: The Moment-by-Moment Process.* New York: Guilford Press.

Heidegger, M. (1963). *Being and Time.* New York: Harper & Row.

Klagsbrun, J. (1999). Focusing, Illness, and Healthcare. *The Folio: A Journal for Focusing and Experiential Therapy,* Vol. 18, No.1. pp. 162-170.

Klein, J. (1999). *The Interactive Method: The Path of Healing Through Empathy and Compassion.* Combined Edition. The Center for Compassionate Empathic Communication. 62 North Lakeshore Drive, Hypoluxo, Fl. 33462.

Klein, J. (2001). *Interactive Focusing Therapy: Healing Relationships.* The Center for Compassionate Empathic Communication. 62 North Lakeshore Drive, Hypoluxo, Fl. 33462

Klein, M., Mathieu-Coughlan, P., & Kiesler, D. (1986). The Experiencing Scales. In L.S. Greenberg & W.M. Pinsof (Eds.), *The Psychotherapeutic Process: A Research Handbook.* New York: Guilford Press.

Levin, D.M. (1985). *The Body's Recollection of Being.* London: Routledge.

Littlewood, W. (1992) Experiencing Insight: The Aha! Phenomenon. *The Folio: A Journal for Focusing and Experiential Therapy.* Chapters 3 & 4. Spring. Vol. 11, No. 1.

McMahon, E.M. (1993). *Beyond the Myth of Dominance.* Kansas City: Sheed & Ward.

Napier, A.Y. & Whitaker, C.A. (1978). *The Family Crucible.* New York: Harper & Row.

Perls, F.S. (1969). *Gestalt Therapy Verbatim.* California: Real People Press.

Real, T. (1997). *I Don't Want To Talk About It.* New York: Scribner.

Real, T. (2002). *How Can I Get Through To You?* New York: Scribner.

Rogers, C.R. (1951). *Client-Centered Therapy.* Boston: Houghton Mifflin.

Rogers, C.R. (1961). *On Becoming A Person.* Boston: Houghton Mifflin. Rogers.

Rogers, C.R. (Ed.). (1967). The Therapeutic Relationship and Its Impact: A Program of Research in Psychotherapy with Schizophrenics. Wisconsin: University of Wisconsin Press.

Rosenberg, M. (1983). *A Model for Nonviolent Communication.* Philadelphia: New Society Publishers.

Satir, V.M. (1967). *Conjoint Family Therapy.* California: Science and Behavior Books.

Satir, V.M. (1972). *Peoplemaking.* California: Science and Behavior Books.

Weiser, A. (1994). *The Power of Focusing: A Practical Guide to Emotional Self-Healing*. California: New Harbinger.

About the Author

Bala Jaison, Ph.D., is a psychotherapist in private practice for individuals, couples and families, and Director of Focusing for Creative Living in Toronto, a Gov't Recognized Educational Institution providing leading-edge training for therapists, educators, business and medical professionals. She has developed the innovative therapy approach, Solution Oriented Focusing Therapy (SOFT), integrating the models of Solution Focused and Focusing Oriented Psychotherapy, which she currently teaches to therapists in North America and abroad. She is a Certifying Coordinator for the International Focusing Institute, co-editor of the Folio, the academic journal of the International Focusing Institute, and has written extensively on the clinical applications of Focusing in therapy. Her book has been translated into Spanish by publishers Desclée De Brouwer (www.edesclee.com) and Dutch by Uitgeverij De Toorts (www.toorts.nl).

Contact information:

Bala Jaison: balaj@sympatico.ca
The Focusing Institute: www.focusing.org
The Brief Therapy Network: www.brieftherapynetwork.com
Canada : www.cavershambooksellers.com
Worldwide: www.amazon.com